ANDRE' MOORE

Scripturally Can Women Use Public Platforms To Teach Men The Gospel of Christ?

Examining: God's Implementing of "As Also Saith The Law"

First published by Andre' Moore 2025

Copyright © 2025 by Andre' Moore

All rights reserved. No part of this publication may be reproduced, stored or transmitted in any form or by any means, electronic, mechanical, photocopying, recording, scanning, or otherwise without written permission from the publisher. It is illegal to copy this book, post it to a website, or distribute it by any other means without permission.

Andre' Moore asserts the moral right to be identified as the author of this work.

King James Version Bible verses are in the public domain. All original additions including all chapters with their chapter summaries are copyright 2025.

First edition

ISBN: 979-8-218-75551-5

This book was professionally typeset on Reedsy. Find out more at reedsy.com

Contents

1 As Also Saith The Law	1
1 Corinthians 14:27-35	4
1 Timothy 2:8-15	8
Scriptural Implementation	13
2 Phoebe and Junia	17
Junia	33
Who Qualified To Be An Apostle?	34
The Capability of The Apostles	42
What is said of Junia and Andronicus in Romans 16:7	48
3 Galatians 3:28: Ye Are All One in Christ	52
What is the context of the statement in Galatians 3:28?	53
Does The Context Reference a Law Prior to Christ?	63
Does The Conclusion Drawn Contradict Other Scriptures?	64
How Does God Implement Galatians 3:28?	76
4 Company of Prophets/Sons of The Prophets	78
5 The Prophetesses of Scripture	98
Miriam	99
Deborah	113
Deborah - A Judge and Prophetess	115
Huldah and Priscillia	120
The Functioning Law System in the Foundation of the Lord's church	124
The Omission of Deborah in 1 Samuel 12:11 & Hebrews 11:32	126
Executing of Burnt Offerings	127

Divine Order	130
6 Women Who Labored in the Temple and the Gospel of Christ	135
Anna The Prophetess	135
Euodias and Syntyche	138
Philip's Four Daughters Who Prophesied	143
7 The Patriarchal Age	148
8 The Law of Moses	164
The Example For Modern Media	169
9 Background To The Leviticial Priesthood	186
Conclusion	198
Appendix	199
The Hebrew Word Mashal Used For Public Authority	199

1

As Also Saith The Law

An excellent brother in Christ and instructor within World Video Bible School by the name of Chuck Horner once made the statement that, whether he was sleeping or awake, he would be teaching the Gospel to someone somewhere in the world. As his videos taught people the Gospel, they were recorded, and many interested souls in various time zones around the world learned by watching his lessons. Bro. Chuck Horner has gone to be with the Lord now, but another brother in Christ named Rudy Cain made a tremendous statement concerning Bro. Chuck Horner upon his departure from this life: the statement, **"Even in his death, he will continue to teach the Bible to thousands in the years to come."** His videos teaching sound doctrine will still be in use for however long the Lord desires. There is a reason I make this statement, which will be known later in this writing.

A lot has been said among the Lord's church regarding women using public platforms to teach the Gospel of our Lord and Savior Jesus Christ. Is it permitted for women to teach men publicly? Are the commands that we find in Scripture only limited to the church and the worship service of our Lord? The focal point of the questions at hand centers around two sets of Scriptures: the commands we find both in 1 Corinthians 14:27-35 and 1 Timothy 2:8-15, which we will discuss in further detail. Let us first briefly draw attention to the necessity of every Christian to spread the Gospel when physically capable of doing so.

Spreading the gospel is called upon every individual who has put on Christ. We know that an individual puts on Christ in baptism, as the Scriptures teach. One of the many examples found in Scripture is Galatians 3:27 KJV:

"For as many of you as have been baptized into Christ have put on Christ."

Once an individual has become a follower of Jesus Christ, we can utilize what is widely known as the Great Commission given by our Lord and Savior Jesus Christ, found in Matthew 28:19-20 KJV:

"Go ye therefore, and teach all nations, baptizing them in the name of the Father, and of the Son, and of the Holy Ghost: Teaching them to observe all things whatsoever I have commanded you: and, lo, I am with you alway, even unto the end of the world. Amen."

This statement made by Jesus, to whom all power was given, grants the Christian the authority to teach the gospel of Jesus Christ, by His scriptural standard, to all men everywhere. The necessity lies in the fact that, as Scripture tells us in Acts 17:31 KJV:

"He hath appointed a day, in the which He will judge the world in righteousness by that man whom He hath ordained; whereof He hath given assurance unto all men, in that He hath raised Him from the dead."

There is a great day of judgment on which Christ will judge the world. Let us look a little closer at the statements made by Jesus in Matthew 28:19-20. In examining the text at hand within the Gospel account of Matthew, we first need to acknowledge that there are specific audiences being addressed. First, Matthew is writing about an audience to whom Jesus is speaking directly; second, Matthew is directly addressing this letter specifically to the Jews. This is evident in the fact that Matthew gives the Jewish genealogy of Jesus at the beginning of his letter in Matthew chapter 1, something that the Jews would primarily know. Third, Matthew's writing also addresses the entire world, including future generations, which includes you and me.

Let us focus on the audience to whom Jesus is speaking directly, with the text at hand, because oftentimes the requirements of the text can be understood, but the details of the text can be overlooked. As we highlight Jesus' direct audience in Matthew 28:19-20, I call your attention to the previous three verses, beginning from verse 16 as Matthew 28:16-20 KJV reads:

"Then the eleven disciples went away into Galilee, into a mountain where Jesus had appointed them. And when they saw him, they worshipped him: but some doubted. And Jesus came and spake unto them, saying, all power is given unto me in heaven and in earth. Go ye therefore, and teach all nations, baptizing them in the name of the Father, and of the Son, and of the Holy Ghost: Teaching them to observe all things whatsoever I have commanded you: and, lo, I am with you alway, even unto the end of the world."

We notice that Jesus' direct audience in making this statement is his eleven disciples. Upon studying this text, there are two things worthy of mention. All nations are required to observe the commandments of Jesus. Yet, Jesus specifically charged men that He selected with this task to teach all nations, which included the public platform, as referenced in various scriptures, one of which is Matthew 10:1-27 specifically Matthew 10:27 KJV:

"What I tell you in darkness, that speak ye in light: and what ye hear in the ear, that preach ye upon the housetops."

This is significant for the topic at hand, "Can Women Use Public Platforms To Teach Men the Gospel Of Christ?" **Why did Jesus specifically choose men for this task of public teaching before the establishment of the New Testament church?** To answer this question, let us examine the set of scriptures initially referred to at the onset of this writing, which is the core of the topic at hand.

1 Corinthians 14:27-35

When studying the apostle Paul's first letter to the Corinthians in the scriptures, it is to be acknowledged that this letter was not only addressed to the Corinthians but also as 1 Corinthians 1:2 KJV reads:

"With all that in every place call upon the name of Jesus Christ our Lord."

This alerts us to the fact that what is stated in this letter is also to be followed by every Christian within every church belonging to Christ. Upon studying the first Corinthian letter, we see the Corinthian church infested with many problems. The brethren in the congregation had strife among each other; the congregation was not implementing church discipline, and particularly in 1 Corinthians chapter 14, there was disorder within the worship service. The verses that are of importance to us currently are vv. 27-40; the reason for this is that they outline the specific order that is to be maintained during the worship service, as Paul would go on to say, in 1 Corinthians 14:37 KJV:

"Let him acknowledge that the things that I write unto you are the commandments of the Lord."

The verse at hand, which we are addressing, is found in 1 Corinthians 14:34 KJV:

"Let your women keep silence in the churches: for it is not permitted unto them to speak; but they are commanded to be under obedience, as also saith the law."

Of high importance in this verse is the statement *"as also saith the law."* What law is this? To what extent does this law cover? And how long has it been in existence? The argument is made that this is strictly referring to the order of worship and only applies to worship; however, everything outlined in the context refers to the order of worship from verses 27-40, but specific attention is given to the women in verse 34, as highlighted by comparison to *"as also saith the law."* With these facts considered, the statement *"as also saith the law"* in verse 34 refers to a law that has already been in existence before the church, and the church is to apply this preexisting law in the same way that God has implemented it prior to the establishment of the church.

As we consider the comparison made in verse 34 regarding the subjection of women, as also saith the law, we know this to be based on preexisting law, given the fact that Paul also uses similar language elsewhere in scripture when noting that a preexisting standard is to be applied. For example, Paul says in Romans 1:16-17 KJV:

"For I am not ashamed of the gospel of Christ: for it is the power of God unto salvation to everyone that believeth; to the Jew first, and also

to the Greek. For therein is the righteousness of God revealed from faith to faith: as it is written, the just shall live by faith."

What does Paul mean here when he says ***"from faith to faith: as it is written, the just shall live by faith?"*** First, we point out that Paul is stating that salvation is found in the Gospel of Christ, which is now the righteousness of God. Yet, to prove this point, Paul appeals to the word of God in Old Testament scriptures under the Law of Moses, which also prophesied about the coming of Christ; of which the original statement ***"the just shall live by faith"*** is found in Habakkuk 2:4.

While the prophet Habakkuk prophesied to Israel about the captivity they were about to endure by the hand of the Chaldeans in Habakkuk chapter 1, the Lord tells Habakkuk that the revelation is for an appointed time in chapter 2. Then the Lord makes a contrast in Habakkuk 2:4, with one who is arrogant and not upright, with the just [righteous] living by faith. Even though God was sending Israel into bondage, the commands that God gave Israel in the Law of Moses remained binding for Israel until the coming of Christ; that of which is said in Leviticus 18:5 KJV:

"ye shall therefore keep my statutes and my judgments: which if a man do, he shall live in them."

Obedient faith was still required, evident by the Hebrew word used for faith in Habakkuk 2:4, which is ĕmûnâh 'ĕmûnâh and is defined as faithfulness.

Secondly, by Paul appealing to the words of Habakkuk, he acknowledges that a standard was applied at the time Habakkuk lived, that being to live by faith. Paul's appeal to this standard of living from the Old Testament with the words ***"as it is written"*** means this exact standard is to be applied under the gospel of Christ, evident by the fact that Paul equally applies the standard in Romans 1:17 when he says, *"from faith to faith, as it is written, the just shall live by faith."* The same standard of living obediently which applied to the Law of Moses now applies to living obediently to the gospel of Christ.

Therefore, we confirm that when we look at the comparison made in 1 Corinthians 14:34 with the women and *"as also saith the law,"* we know that the standard with which this law was applied before the Lord's church was established must equally be applied in the Lord's church by the commandment of God (1 Corinthians 14:37). But what is this law?

Let us first explain what *"let your women keep silent in the churches"* means in 1 Corinthians 14:34. Our English word "silent" in this verse is translated from the Greek word *sigao*, which means to keep silence, to hold one's peace, to keep in silence. Keeping in context with the order Paul is commanding, beginning from 1 Corinthians 14:27 and following through to verse 34, the silence is to establish order and authority in the worship service. If there was no interpreter, then the one speaking in a tongue was to keep silent; the same with the prophet, and also the silence of the women in worship. This lets us know the silence that is being talked about here is regarding one of order and authority, as well as leading in worship service, as it pertains to the women in verse 34; subjection must be had. However, the statement is based on a preexisting standard *"as also saith the law"* that was known before the church came into existence. This statement that Paul makes is saying this preexisting law is also to be enforced under the New Covenant (the Gospel of Christ).

Paul does not explain specifically the details of this law in 1 Corinthians

14; so, it is necessary to call on another set of scriptures written by the same holy, inspired apostle Paul that are in harmony with the language used within 1 Corinthians 14:34 to properly understand the statement made in said verse *"as also saith the law."* Additionally, we will use Biblical examples to provide the necessary inference (irresistible truth) that shows the implementation of this law, even in the whole of the Bible itself.

1 Timothy 2:8-15

I would like to first call your attention to 1 Timothy 2:11-14. We find the language used in this set of verses in harmony with the previous verse found in 1 Corinthians 14:34. As 1 Timothy 2:11-14 KJV says:

"Let the woman learn in silence with all submission. But I suffer not a woman to teach or to usurp authority over the man, but to be in silence. For Adam was formed first, then Eve. And Adam was not deceived, but the woman being deceived fell into transgression."

Here in this set of verses, Paul amplifies by way of explanation the preexisting law mentioned in 1 Corinthians 14:34. In examining the two sets of verses, once again, 1 Corinthians 14:34 KJV says:

"Let your women keep silence in the churches: for it is not permitted unto them to speak; but they are commanded to be under obedience, as also saith the law."

Comparing the required subjection of women to the preexisting *"as also saith the law,"* here in 1 Timothy 2:11-14, Paul says the same thing regarding the silence and subjection of the woman, but now he uses a

Greek primary particle, critical for this discussion—the Greek word *"gar,"* defined as giving a reason to the previous statement; which is translated to our English word "for" in 1 Timothy 2:13. This means Paul is now explaining the reason for the required subjection. For the factual reason that the same silence is required of women in 1 Corinthians 14:34 as in 1 Timothy 2:11-14, it goes to show that the explanation given in 1 Timothy 2:11-14 is the law referenced in the statement seen in 1 Corinthians 14:34, *"as also saith the law,"* of which we have established above is a law that was preexisting before the establishment of the church. This set of verses concludes that this was law from the very beginning, and as God utilized both men and women to implement His law throughout the Scriptures, He has not altered this command He has given to humanity, not even in the slightest.

How is this evidence critical to "Can Women Use Public Platforms to Teach Men the Gospel?" Now that we have established that this law **(that we will now address as the authority/subjection law)**, as discussed in 1 Corinthians 14:34 and 1 Timothy 2:11-14, was preexisting to the establishment of the church, it is extremely important that we consider two things: the context in which the statements are written and how it is implemented throughout the whole of the Bible. We have previously discussed the context of 1 Corinthians 14:27-40, so allow us to now discuss the context of 1 Timothy 2:8-15 and then Biblical implementation.

Let us, first once again, acknowledge the fact that the subjection of women is based on law established from the very beginning of time. Therefore, what is spoken of in the context of 1 Timothy 2 must fit the law throughout the entire Bible. To conclude contrary to this initial law is to conclude outside of God's word. 1 Timothy 2:8-10 KJV reads:
"I will therefore that men pray everywhere, lifting up holy hands,

without wrath and doubting. In like manner also, that women adorn themselves in modest apparel, with shamefacedness and sobriety; not with braided hair, or gold, or pearls, or costly array; but (which becometh women professing godliness) with good works."

The authority/subjection law being addressed within this context does not begin in verse 11 but in verse 8. Paul lets us know that men are to pray in every place; we know this is speaking of worship service, as prayer is a requirement within the Lord's worship service. Yet, this is not limited to the worship service. With the law from the beginning considered, a crucial detail to understand is that *"every where"* is inclusive of every public place. The authority/subjection law is implemented in all public settings, (**as we will see in our next section of Scriptural Implementation**). As we continue in verse 8, wrath and doubting are not publicly acceptable by God under any circumstance, whether in the public setting of worship or any other public setting, as they do not represent God at all.

Additionally, we look at verses 9-10; verse ten declares that what is said in verse nine concerning the women in Christ is a standard that God has implemented for women in the gospel of Christ. When these actions are taken by the women in verse nine, it shows a scriptural declaration of professing godliness with good works in the gospel of Jesus Christ; thereby, women will be holding themselves to the standard of the gospel of Christ. Yet, the term *"in like manner"* in verse nine concerning the women confirms an equality with what is said in verse eight concerning the men. This is done by way of contrast in explaining a standard of good works for each class of individuals discussed in verses eight and nine (i.e., men and women). Thus, the standard of good works discussed in verses eight and nine is to be equally applied by the term *"every where,"* as stated in verse eight.

The question that is asked is: to what extent does everywhere apply? The answer is that it encompasses every location where Christians are to profess godliness with good works in the gospel of Christ, thus *"every where"* where there is a gathering of people for the purpose of the gospel of Christ. The professing of good works made by the action of prayer, which is found in the standard of the gospel of Christ, must be implemented by the Lord's church when the church assembles for worship and is equally implemented by the Lord's church outside of assembled worship, as good works in Christ are to be implemented beyond the bounds of the worship assembly. This is precisely the point that the apostle Paul makes elsewhere in the scriptures as he writes to the saints in Ephesus in Ephesians 2:10 KJV:

"For we are His workmanship, created in Christ Jesus unto good works, which God hath before ordained that we should walk in them."

As Paul makes the point in Ephesians 2 that it is not by works of the Law of Moses that one is saved but by the grace that God has extended to man through His Son Jesus Christ, this lets us know that we are saved by obedience to the teachings in Christ (i.e., good works), not by obedience to the Law of Moses. Two points are evident with this declaration made in Ephesians 2:10.

First, when an individual is created in Christ Jesus (a point also seen in Galatians 6:15), that individual was created to do good works. Thus, whatever the scriptures state as a good work in Christ, a Christian must do them, whether the good works are quantitatively addressing the whole body (every member) or qualitatively addressing a class of the body (men or women).

Second, Paul makes an imperative statement in this verse; that being Christians *"should walk in them."* This statement reflects a way of living, being occupied with the good works in Christ. Thus, Christians are to be occupied with maintaining the good works created in Christ Jesus by living according to His teachings (i.e., the gospel of Christ).

Therefore, it is to be acknowledged that the life of maintaining good works in Christ, seen in Ephesians 2:10, is equivalent to the declaration that is to be had with the women professing godliness with good works in 1 Timothy 2:9-10; a declaration qualitatively for women in Christ to maintain modest apparel with shamefacedness and sobriety, extending beyond the worship setting into all areas of life. Additionally, because what is said of the women in 1 Timothy 2:9-10 is equivalent to what is said of the men in verse eight, by the statement *"in like manner,"* it confirms that the statement made in verse eight requiring the men to pray everywhere also applies outside of worship settings and is to be done in every place. This underscores the authority granted solely to men in praying everywhere there is a gathering of people for the purpose of the gospel of Christ.

Furthermore, as we recognize what is said of the women in vv. 9-10, it must be acknowledged that anything short of the good works that are to be publicly professed by women in this verse, beyond the worship setting, would be a failure to walk in the light as He is in the light, as stated in 1 Jn. 1:7, placing the Christian woman in a state of sin. Equally, men who neglect to lead in prayer in various settings beyond the worship setting, where both men and women are present, will do the same. In concluding this section, we look at 1 Timothy 2:15 KJV:

"Notwithstanding she shall be saved in childbearing, if they continue in faith and charity and holiness with sobriety."

Of importance in this verse is the Greek primary particle *"deh"* (Notwithstanding), simply defined as moreover (i.e., more information is being disclosed); this term is adversative to what is said in verse 14, showing importance in the generalization of the term woman and how she is preserved, as stated in verse 15 (applying to the woman in all settings). This means this applies to all women in general, as pertaining to the authority/subjection law, which Paul confirms was from the beginning, and as stated within this context, is applied generally to men and women, not just to the worship service of the Lord's church.

Scriptural Implementation

Now that we have scripturally and contextually addressed the two sets of scriptures at the core of the topic at hand, let us examine the scriptural implementation of this specific law. What I mean by this is that now we have established that the authority/subjection law talked about in 1 Corinthians 14:34 and 1 Timothy 2:8-15 is a law dealing with both the public worship assembly and every public platform, which was initiated in the beginning with Adam and Eve. Let us see how God Himself puts His law into action, as He gives man His word. As we consider these accounts, it is important to utilize the standard of necessary inference (irresistible truth). Meaning, that with how the law has been scripturally outlined in this discussion, the forthcoming accounts will draw the **unavoidable truth** that this authority/subjection law must be applied.

The first case that I call your attention to is found in Acts 1:15-26. In Acts 1:15-26, Judas' office was commanded to be filled, as was prophesied by David in the Old Testament, as referenced in Psalm 69:25 KJV:

"Let their habitation be desolate; and let none dwell in their tents,"

And Psalm 109:8 KJV:
"Let his days be few, and let another take his office."

Why was the command specifically for a man to replace Judas' office as an apostle? Careful consideration of Acts 1:21-22 stresses Divine necessity by the Greek word *"dei"* (**must; necessary**); which means a man replacing Judas was required within Divine law, which is confirmed by Peter in Acts 1:20 KJV:

"For it is written in the book of Psalms, let his habitation be desolate and let no man dwell therein: and his bishoprick let another take."

If the command was for a man in Acts 1:15-26 to publicly proclaim Christ before the establishment of the church, and we see that Jesus specifically selected all men to be His apostles in the gospel accounts, then by necessary inference (irresistible truth), the command was for Jesus to select all men to publicly teach the gospel. What we see in this set of verses definitively meets the standard of *"as also saith the law"* regarding the Scriptural Implementing of the authority/subjection law.

Mark 3:14 KJV states:
"And he ordained twelve, that they should be with him, and that he might send them forth to preach."

The apostles were to be the public criers (heralds), to publish and proclaim openly the gospel; Luke 6:13 KJV states:
"And when it was day, he called unto him his disciples: and of them he chose twelve, whom also he named apostles; Simon, (whom he also named Peter,) and Andrew his brother, James and John, Philip and Bartholomew, Matthew and Thomas, James the son of Alphaeus, and

Simon called Zelotes, and Judas the brother of James, and Judas Iscariot, which also was the traitor."

What law is Jesus following, which is implied by the force of command being used in Acts 1:21-22, which necessarily infers a command for Jesus to select men, as shown in our verses in Mark and Luke; which was enforced before the church, was used in the founding of the church, and is still in existence during the era of the church?

I now bring you back to the beginning of this discussion in which the question was posed: **Why did Jesus specifically choose men for this task of public teaching before the establishment of the New Testament church?** As we look back to Matthew 28:16-20, we can now confirm, based on the law that was given, that the command was for the men to publicly teach the gospel to all nations, which includes the authority/subjection commands we find in 1 Corinthians 14:34 and 1 Timothy 2:11-14, instructing how the women are to conduct themselves both in the worship setting and the public setting **based on how even Jesus Himself implements the authority/subjection law.**

This is why we see men strictly selected to publicly proclaim the gospel, part of which included going into the marketplace to teach, as we see the apostle Paul does in Acts 17:17-19. The law that was established at the beginning is implemented throughout the Scriptures, even with the Bible as a whole. In introducing the topic at hand, I mentioned an excellent brother in Christ by the name of Chuck Horner, who has now departed this life and is with the Lord. The statement Brother Rudy Cain made concerning the sound teaching that Chuck Horner committed himself to was, **"Even in his death, he will continue to teach the Bible to thousands in the years to come."** This is a tremendous statement that also applies to the writers of the entire Bible, men whom God Himself chose; even in their death, they continue to teach God's word publicly to the entire world until the end of all time!

It was mentioned earlier that there are three audiences in Matthew's gospel account; the readers of God's word today are that third audience, of which every man whom God has used to write His word is still publicly teaching (and will remain publicly teaching) the entire world, even in death. We know that God has specifically chosen men to write His word, as Scripture confirms in 2 Peter 1:20-21 KJV:

"Knowing this first, that no prophecy of the scripture is of any private interpretation. For the prophecy came not in old time by the will of man: but holy men of God spake as they were moved by the Holy Ghost."

God Himself is following the law that He gave from the beginning with public teaching, which has endured and will endure forever (1 Peter 1:24-25). As we continue in this book, we will expound through examination God's implementation of the authority/subjection law, with its origin in the beginning with God's creation of man and woman and seen throughout the whole canon of Scripture.

2

Phoebe and Junia

To begin, let us look at Romans 16:1-2 KJV:

"I commend unto you Phebe our sister, which is a servant of the church which is at Cenchrea:

That ye receive her in the Lord, as becometh saints, and that ye assist her in whatsoever business she hath need of you: for she hath been a succourer of many, and of myself also."

There's a popular thought, when the pages of scripture stop at Romans 16:1-2, that Phoebe was a deaconess (a recognized official leader) in the Lord's church, by Paul's acknowledgment of Phoebe as a **servant** of the church at Cenchrea. The word "servant" in the English language is the definition of the word ***diakonos*** in the original language, so the thought is that Paul, an inspired writer of God's word, acknowledges Phoebe as a deacon (***diakonos***). In the scriptures, the word ***diakonos*** is used several times and in either one of two ways: ***diakonos*** can be used in a technical way, which is an official use of the word; therefore, the scriptures will tell us the qualifications of holding this office or will indicate if certain individuals or a group of individuals have met those qualifications. ***Diakonos*** can also be used in a non-technical way, which simply describes something or someone who is serving a specific task without mention of qualifications met for an official office. When determining if ***diakonos*** is being used as a technical term with an official use rather than a non-technical term without an official use, the context must demand the technical use of the word ***diakonos***, with the official qualifications shown to be laid out or met by the said individual or group of individuals. As we begin to examine Phoebe, we will take a close look at the word "servant" in the context of Paul's writing to those in Rome; we will see how the scriptures implement the use of this word in each instance that it's used in Romans, and the scriptures will direct us to how this applies to Phoebe.

Before we look at the word "servant" within its context in Romans, as previously mentioned, it pertains to the word ***diakonos.*** The scriptures will show us within the context if a demand for the technical use of the word has been met, with the official qualifications laid out for the office in the said scripture or if a certain individual or group of individuals is shown to have met those qualifications through the demand of the context in which the statement is written. For example, in Philippians 1:1 KJV:

"Paul and Timotheus, the servants of Jesus Christ, to all the saints in Christ Jesus which are at Philippi, with the bishops and deacons."

In Paul's introduction to the Philippians, he addresses the entire congregation; Paul addresses all of the saints first, yet he specifically mentions individuals who are included with the saints at Philippi that hold an office: *"**bishops and deacons.**"* In this verse, deacons hold the same quality of meeting a specific standard as the bishops; we know this to be true by the primary particle that is used to connect the two, the word *"**and.**"* Thus, showing that since the saints classified as bishops met a specific standard to hold this office, the saints also classified as deacons equally had to meet a specific standard for holding the office of a deacon within the congregation at Philippi. Furthermore, the clear distinction of the bishops and deacons from the rest of the saints in this verse verifies qualifications have been met to classify these saints as such at Philippi. Therefore, since these scriptures use a standard of qualifications based on the distinctions made by Paul, we must examine those standards of qualifications as we discuss when the technical term for ***diakonos*** must be applied to the word within the context. Therefore, we will examine the scriptures where these qualifications are laid out for the Lord's church. The said individual **must** meet the qualifications of holding that office as laid out for the church within the scriptures, seen in 1 Timothy 3:1-12 KJV:

"This is a true saying, if a man desire the office of a bishop, he desireth a good work.

A bishop then must be blameless, the husband of one wife, vigilant, sober, of good behaviour, given to hospitality, apt to teach; not given to wine, no striker, not greedy of filthy lucre; but patient, not a brawler, not covetous; one that ruleth well his own house, having his children in subjection with all gravity; (For if a man know not how to rule his own house, how shall he take care of the church of God?) Not a novice, lest being lifted up with pride he fall into the condemnation of the devil. Moreover he must have a good report of them which are without; lest he fall into reproach and the snare of the devil. Likewise must the deacons (diakonos) *be grave, not doubletongued, not given to much wine, not greedy of filthy lucre; Holding the mystery of the faith in a pure conscience. And let these also first be proved; then let them use the office of a deacon, being found blameless. Even so must their wives be grave, not slanderers, sober, faithful in all things. Let the deacons be the husbands of one wife, ruling their children and their own houses well."*

As we are discussing when to use the technical term ***diakonos***, denoting an individual has met the qualifications to hold this office, I specifically call your attention to 1 Timothy 3:2 and 1 Timothy 3:12. In verse 2, the qualifications to be a bishop are that one must be blameless, the husband of one wife, vigilant, sober, of good behavior, given to hospitality, and apt to teach; this word "must" is the Greek word ***Dei***, which by definition means it is absolutely necessary as binding; it is the same word that we've discussed and seen used for the fulfillment of scripture and the selection of the apostle to replace Judas in Acts 1:16-22. Furthermore, individuals desiring to work as bishops must meet all of the commands outlined for bishops in 1 Timothy 3 to be qualified to hold this office in the Lord's church. In particular, he must be the husband of one wife. In like manner, individuals desiring to work as deacons in the Lord's church must meet all the commands outlined in these verses where they are mentioned to be qualified for the office of a deacon. Therefore, as we've looked at Philippians 1:1 where bishops and deacons are distinctly mentioned with all the saints at Philippi, we know according to the scriptures that these men in Philippi met the qualifications listed in 1 Timothy 3, as Paul stated in 1 Timothy 3:15 KJV:

"That thou mayest know how thou oughtest to behave thyself in the house of God, which is the church of the living God, the pillar and ground of the truth."

However, there are some who will look at 1 Timothy 3:11 and take note of the fact that this verse says *"even so wives be grave not slanders, sober, faithful in all things"* as evidence of equivalent qualifications for women to be deacons as well; yet, there are two facts that disqualify this idea. First, as we look at the very next verse, Paul makes an imperative statement in verse 12; meaning it is an authoritative command, evident by the use of the Greek word ***estō estōsan*** [be], *"let the deacons be*

husbands of one wife." It is required for deacons to be husbands of one wife. The second fact is that what is mentioned in verse 11 pertaining to the wives is a standard of qualification for the husbands under consideration for the office, as being evident of the husband ruling his own house well, as seen in verse 12. Furthermore, what is required of the wife in verse 11 is required of all Christians. All Christians are required to be faithful in all things, honest, sober, and not slanderers, as this is a part of the gospel of Christ.

Now that we've established what qualifies the use of "deacon" as a technical term is meeting the qualifications listed in 1 Timothy 3 and that the context will reveal if the qualifications have been met; we will now examine the word "servant" (***diakonos***) with its use in the context of the Roman epistle, beginning with its first use in Romans 13:1-5, with emphasis on Romans 13:4 KJV:

"Let every soul be subject unto the higher powers. For there is no power but of God: the powers that be are ordained of God. Whosoever therefore resisteth the power, resisteth the ordinance of God: and they that resist shall receive to themselves damnation. For rulers are not a terror to good works, but to the evil. Wilt thou then not be afraid of the power? do that which is good, and thou shalt have praise of the same: For he is the minister of God to thee for good. But if thou do that which is evil, be afraid; for he beareth not the sword in vain: for he is the minister of God, a revenger to execute wrath upon him that doeth evil. Wherefore ye must needs be subject, not only for wrath, but also for conscience sake."

There is an imperative in the statements of Paul in these verses that Christians are to be subject to governing authorities, the reason being that governing authorities are appointed by God. Therefore, to resist the power of the governing authorities is to resist the instrumentality of God's usage of them. It must be noted that we are to be subject to the governing authorities as long as they do not go against our requirement to obey God; in such a case, we are to do as the statements of Peter and the other apostles in Acts 5:29 KJV:

"Then Peter and the other apostles answered and said, We ought to obey God rather than men."

As we continue to examine the text under consideration in Romans 13, it is further stated in Romans 13:3 that the rulers which make up these governing authorities are to be a terror to evil. As we realize that God uses the governing authorities and the rulers within them as His instruments to punish evil, I now call your attention to Romans 13:4. Regarding the governing authorities, specific mention is made in verse 4 that they are:

"The minister of God to thee for good" and *"he is the minister of God, a revenger to execute wrath upon him that doeth evil."*

The word minister in this verse is the Greek word (***diakonos***), which is our word under consideration in Romans 16:1 with Phoebe, as its definition is servant. As we've scripturally examined, the context will reveal if the technical use of the term deacon is to be applied as holding the office of a deacon in the Lord's church as outlined in 1 Timothy 3. The governing authorities are what is under consideration in Romans 13:1-5, which is an entity or governing body, making it separate from the Lord's church. What is outlined in 1 Timothy 3 are the qualifications for individual men under consideration for the office of bishop and deacon within the Lord's church, not for a collective body being used outside of His church. Therefore, in Romans 13:1-5, the technical use of the term deacon, though translated as minister, cannot apply to the governing authorities discussed; however, we see the governing authorities serving a specific purpose by God in the fact that Paul says they are *"the minister of God to thee for good"* and *"he is the minister of God, a revenger to execute wrath upon him that doeth evil."* The reasoning given by Paul as to why we are to be subject to the governing authorities lets us know this is their sole purpose of instrumentality by God in being His servant.

Additionally, I call your attention to Romans 13:6 KJV:

"For for this cause pay ye tribute also: for they are God's ministers, attending continually upon this very thing."

With the governing authorities as God's servants, we are required by the standard of God to be subject to them, not only for wrath but also for conscience' sake. For this reason, we are to pay tribute (also known as taxes). Specifically, I call your attention to ministers in this verse; though the same governing authorities are being addressed, it is not the Greek word **diakonos** or servant as mentioned in verse 4. The Greek word used here is **leitourgos**, which is defined as a public servant. The entity of governing authorities is continually a public servant of God, for the sake of being *"the minister of God to thee for good"* and *"he is the minister of God, a revenger to execute wrath upon him that doeth evil."* God publicly uses the governing authorities for all people; as God reigns over the nations, God sits on His holy throne (Psalm 47:8). Of importance in the usage of the Greek word **leitourgos** is that this word is also mentioned of the apostle Paul, when translated as minister in Romans 15:16 KJV:

"That I should be the minister of Jesus Christ to the Gentiles, ministering the gospel of God, that the offering up of the Gentiles might be acceptable, being sanctified by the Holy Ghost."

The apostle Paul was a public servant of Jesus Christ to the Gentiles. Gentiles were known as a race of people or nations distinctly separate from the Jews because of that barrier of dividing wall known as the Law of Moses (Ephesians 2:11-15). His public service of the gospel of God was preaching the gospel, which resulted in the obedience of the Gentiles in word and deed, as mentioned in Romans 15:18 KJV:

"For I will not presume to speak of anything except what Christ has accomplished through me, resulting in the obedience of the Gentiles by word and deed."

There are two facts to acknowledge with this information in mind. First, Paul publicly ministering the gospel of God to the Gentiles lets us know that the gospel, with its laws, rewards, and instruction therein, is for all of mankind, regardless of race, nationality, gender, or social status; our point of emphasis being the core topic of discussion *"as also saith the law"* in 1 Corinthians 14:34 and 2 Timothy 2:11-14 is to be acknowledged by all as standard in the Lord's church in word and deed. Second, Paul, in his role as an apostle, did for the Gentiles what all of the apostles did; the specific apostle in mind is Peter. In Paul's writing to the Galatians, he mentions in Galatians 2:7-9 KJV:

"But on the contrary, seeing that I had been entrusted with the gospel to the uncircumcised, just as Peter had been to the circumcised. (For He who effectually worked for Peter in his apostleship to the circumcised effectually worked for me also to the Gentiles), And recognizing the grace that had been given to me, James and Cephas and John, who were reputed to be pillars, gave to me and Barnabas the right hand of fellowship, that we might go to the Gentiles, and they to the circumcised."

Paul, in his public service of Jesus Christ in his role as an apostle to the Gentiles (uncircumcision), did nothing different from Peter in his public service of Jesus Christ in his role as an apostle to the Jews (circumcision). One of the requirements of this public service of Jesus

Christ in apostleship was for the individual to be male, as we will further discuss with Junia. However, now we will examine the second use of the term *diakonos* in Romans, which is seen in Romans 15:8 KJV:

"Now I say that Jesus Christ was a minister of the circumcision for the truth of God, to confirm the promises made unto the fathers."

The word minister in this verse is our English word servant or the Greek word *diakonos*, and here it is applied to Jesus Christ. To be correct in applying the technical use of the term *diakonos* to Jesus Christ in this verse, what we know about Jesus Christ within the context must reveal if He met the standard of qualifications as outlined in 1 Timothy 3 for His church. What we know about Jesus Christ in this verse is conveyed in His very name of Christ, meaning "Anointed," Messiah, and Son of God; He is the head of His church. The Messiah, as promised to the fathers and prophesied through the prophets in the Old Testament, was promised to be a blessing to all nations (Genesis 12:3; Gentiles included, Galatians 3:8), to rule the nations with an iron rod (Psalm 2:7-9), to be called Wonderful Counselor, Mighty God, Eternal Father, Prince of Peace (Isaiah 9:6), and to speak of His death, burial, and resurrection (Psalm 16:8-10; Acts 2:25-32). Furthermore, Jesus Christ came to build His church, which was established on the day of Pentecost after His resurrection and ascension to the right hand of God the Father; the church was not established prior to this event. He lived under the Law of Moses and perfectly obeyed it to His death. Additionally, Jesus Christ also said of Himself in John 5:36 KJV:

"For the works which the Father hath given me to finish, the same works that I do, bear witness of me, that the Father hath sent me."

Jesus Christ did nothing less nor more than what the Father sent Him to do. Therefore, according to the scriptures, Christ did not have a wife nor children, and the church, for which He gives instruction for all to behave in and is the head of, was not established while He was living on Earth to meet the standard of qualifications as outlined in 1 Timothy 3; thus, applying the technical use of the term ***diakonos*** to Him. Yet, Jesus Christ was a servant (***diakonos***), and the context explains who He was a servant to and for what purpose He was a servant.

Paul explains that Jesus Christ was a minister of the circumcision and, as we've previously seen, the Jews are the circumcision. Therefore, He was a servant of the Jews. This statement is no different from what Jesus Christ said of Himself while fulfilling His earthly ministry. Jesus said in Matthew 15:24 KJV:

"But he answered and said, I am not sent but unto the lost sheep of the house of Israel."

After giving His disciples power over unclean spirits to cast them out and to heal all manner of sickness and all manner of disease, He told them not to go to the Gentiles or the Samaritans, but rather to the lost sheep of the house of Israel, as stated in Matthew 10:5-6 KJV:

"These twelve Jesus sent forth, and commanded them, saying, Go not into the way of the Gentiles, and into any city of the Samaritans enter ye not: But go rather to the lost sheep of the house of Israel."

Additionally, keep in mind what Jesus Christ said of Himself in John 5:36 KJV:

"For the works which the Father hath given me to finish, the same works that I do, bear witness of me, that the Father hath sent me."

This confirms the Father sent Jesus in His earthly ministry to be a servant to the Jews, as stated in Romans 15:8, thus showing a sole purpose in Jesus Christ as He served the Jews while He was living on

Earth; further confirming the non-technical use of the word ***diakonos***. Jesus Christ was a servant with a specific purpose, and this purpose is further seen in the concluding statement of Romans 15:8, which was ***"to confirm the promises made unto the fathers."*** These promises are also seen in the apostle Paul's statements in Galatians 3:16-17 KJV:

"Now to Abraham and his seed were the promises made. He saith not, And to seeds, as of many; but as of one, And to thy seed, which is Christ. And this I say, that the covenant, that was confirmed before of God in Christ, the law, which was four hundred and thirty years after, cannot disannul, that it should make the promise of none effect."

Jesus Christ, though a servant to the Jews, was the fulfillment of God's promise made to Abraham that Gentiles would have the opportunity for salvation; this evidence is seen in the Old Testament while confirmed in the New Testament. Three sets of scripture confirm this: Galatians 3:8 KJV:

"And the scripture, foreseeing that God would justify the heathen through faith, preached before the gospel unto Abraham, saying, In thee shall all nations be blessed."

Genesis 18:18 KJV:

"Seeing that Abraham shall surely become a great and mighty nation, and all the nations of the earth shall be blessed in him."

And the very next verse following Romans 15:8: Romans 15:9 KJV:

"And that the Gentiles might glorify God for his mercy; as it is written, For this cause I will confess to thee among the Gentiles, and sing unto thy name."

The sole purpose of Jesus Christ being a ***diakonos*** (servant) was to bring the opportunity of salvation for the entire human race, regardless of ethnicity, gender, or social status. Jesus Christ, being the promised seed of Abraham by God the Father, came from the Israel nation and offered the gospel to the Israel nation first, but the gospel was not limited to the Israel nation; it was briefly delayed to the Samaritans and Gentiles and then fully extended to the entire human race, as seen in Acts 8:14 with Samaria receiving the word of God and in Acts 10 - 11:1 with the Gentiles also receiving the word of God.

Thus far, we've seen governing authorities are a servant (***diakonos***) of God, and Jesus Christ was a servant (***diakonos***) to the Jews. In both cases, a specific task serves as the purpose for which each is being used as a servant. Similarly, of high importance is a specific fact mentioned about Paul, seen in Romans 15:25 KJV:

"But now I go unto Jerusalem to minister unto the saints."

Paul made the statement that he was going to Jerusalem to minister (***diakoneo***) or, by definition of the word, to **serve** the saints. Though Paul did not use the word ***diakonos***, he did use the same word from 1 Timothy 3:10;13 to describe what the ***diakonos*** (servant) does and who the ***diakonos*** (servant) is, which is to serve (***diakoneo***). In other words, this word is used interchangeably with ***diakonos*** in the context of 1 Timothy 3 in describing the standard of qualifications to become a deacon in the Lord's church. 1 Timothy 3:10 KJV:

"And let these also first be proved; then let them use the office of a deacon (diakoneo)**, being found blameless."**

And 1 Timothy 3:13 KJV:

"For they that have used the office of a deacon (diakoneo) **well purchase to themselves a good degree, and great boldness in the faith which is in Christ Jesus."**

As the office of a deacon is under consideration with the terms diakonos and diakoneo used interchangeably, understanding how the words are used within the context of the epistle is important to know when the technical terms for the office of a deacon are being used. There is an example in scripture where both words are generically used within the same verse, such as in John 12:26 KJV:

"If any man serve (diakoneo) *me, let him follow me; and where I am, there shall also my servant* (diakonos) *be: if any man serve* (diakoneo) *me, him will my Father honour."*

In the verse just mentioned, anyone who follows Jesus will be known as one who is a servant of Jesus when the commitment is made to serve Him. Here, the office of deacon is not under consideration, as this statement is applied to any man committing to serve Jesus, therefore being added to His church. Yet, any man being added to the Lord's church does not hold the office of deacon because there is a standard of qualifications. Qualifications for this office in His church are not discussed in this statement; therefore, this statement does not meet the standard for one to hold the position as outlined in 1 Timothy 3, thereby showing the generic use of each term in this verse.

Since ***diakonos*** and ***diakoneo*** are used interchangeably in 1 Timothy 3 for the standard of qualifications for a deacon, and this is the only place in the scriptures where this office with its qualifications is discussed in detail; whenever someone is being assigned this office in scripture, the standard laid out in 1 Timothy 3 **must** be applied when the office is being considered where the terms are used.

Yet, as Paul applies this word to himself in Romans 15:25, we know that Paul did not meet the qualifications to become a deacon; simply by the statements that he made of himself describing his marital status specifically in 1 Corinthians 9:2-5 and verse 12 KJV:

"If I be not an apostle unto others, yet doubtless I am to you: for the seal of mine apostleship are ye in the Lord. Mine answer to them that do examine me is this, have we not power to eat and to drink? Have we not power to lead about a sister, a wife, as well as other apostles, and as the brethren of the Lord, and Cephas?"

1 Corinthians 9:12 KJV:

"If others be partakers of this power over you, are not we rather? Nevertheless we have not used this power; but suffer all things, lest we should hinder the gospel of Christ."

Paul said of himself that he had the right to lead a sister as a wife, but he did not, so that he would not hinder the gospel of Christ. Therefore, though Paul used the term applied to a deacon in Romans 15:25, the technical use of the term cannot apply to Paul by the measure of his own statements compared to the standard of qualifications outlined in 1 Timothy 3. So how was Paul a ***diakoneo*** to the saints in Jerusalem in Romans 15:25? Paul explains how in the very next three verses of Romans 15:26-28 KJV:

"For it hath pleased them of Macedonia and Achaia to make a certain contribution for the poor saints which are at Jerusalem. It hath pleased them verily; and their debtors they are. For if the Gentiles have been made partakers of their spiritual things, their duty is also to minister unto them in carnal things. When therefore I have performed this, and have sealed to them this fruit, I will come by you into Spain."

Paul said of himself in Romans 15:28 that he was performing a specific task; this task, as stated in verses 26-27, was to bring the contribution from the saints in Macedonia and Achaia to give to the poor saints in Jerusalem. Within the context of the Romans epistle, Paul's bringing the contribution to Jerusalem is the sole and definitive way that he was a ***diakoneo*** to the saints in Jerusalem, and it leaves no room for any other interpretation as Paul makes the statement that he was to complete this service and *"come by you into Spain."*

Now that we have examined ***diakonos*** as well as ***diakoneo*** as they are used in the context of the Roman epistle, we come back to Romans 16:1-2 KJV:

"I commend unto you Phebe our sister, which is a servant of the church which is at Cenchrea:

That ye receive her in the Lord, as becometh saints, and that ye assist her in whatsoever business she hath need of you: for she hath been a succourer of many, and of myself also."

As we continue our examination, we see Phoebe, as she is called servant (***diakonos***), **does not** meet the standard of qualifications outlined in 1 Timothy 3, where the only place the office with its qualifications is discussed. Therefore, the office with its qualifications explained in 1 Timothy 3 **cannot** be assigned to Phoebe in Romans 16:1-2. Yet, as we see Phoebe being called by the term servant, it consistently flows with the term's usage in all of Romans as we've discussed; thereby showing Paul is not addressing Phoebe as a recognized official leader in the Lord's church. Phoebe had a specific purpose in being a servant of the church at Cenchrea, and in verse 2, an explanation is given with the usage of the Greek word **"Gar,"** which is our English word "for," as to why the saints in Rome are to receive and help this sister, and that is as Paul said *"she hath been a succourer* (helper) *of many and of myself also."* The specific purpose that Phoebe had in being a servant was assisting many, even Paul himself. An important point of emphasis is Phoebe was a helper to Paul; to assign the office of deacon as we've discussed requires the qualifications in 1 Timothy 3. Yet, Paul does not meet those qualifications but applied the interchangeable term for deacon, as seen in 1 Timothy 3:10, 13 to himself in Romans 15:25 while he served the poor saints at Jerusalem, a task he expected to perform and complete. Therefore, showing the help that Paul was to the poor saints at Jerusalem was equivalent to the help that Phoebe was to Paul, and equally she was a consistent help to many as the word servant applied to Phoebe was present tense.

Yet some will contend that according to what is said about Phoebe in Romans 16:2 of her being a succourer of many, including Paul, it shows that she did have authority and because she most likely carried the letter to those in Rome, she preached it to those in the congregations in Rome. First, in order to take this position of Phoebe having authority because she was a helper of many, including Paul, one must equally say that she had authority over Paul as well. We know this to be erroneous as we rightly divide the scriptures because Paul, as an apostle of our Lord and Saviour Jesus Christ, did not have anyone with authority over him except for Jesus, who specifically chose him to be one of His apostles.

Second, to say that Phoebe preached this letter to the churches in Rome violates other scriptures that Paul has written, specifically our core scriptures at the heart of this topic seen in 1 Corinthians 14:34 *"as also saith the law"* and 1 Timothy 2:11-15. Additionally, I call your attention to the fact that what Paul wrote to those in Corinth applied to all congregations of the Lord, as Paul begins 1 Corinthians by saying this in 1 Corinthians 1:2 KJV:

"Unto the church of God which is at Corinth, to them that are sanctified in Christ Jesus, called to be saints, with all that in every place call upon the name of Jesus Christ our Lord, both theirs and ours."

In Paul's introduction of 1 Corinthians, he not only addresses the congregation at Corinth, but he also addresses all in every place that call on the name of Jesus Christ our Lord, in other words, all Christians. We also see him saying in 1 Corinthians 14:33 KJV:

"For God is not the author of confusion, but of peace, as in all churches of the saints."

Furthermore, as we've discussed, the law found in 1 Corinthians 14:34 is fully explained in 1 Timothy 2:11-15, which this book has thoroughly covered from Genesis to the Gospel of Christ. Therefore, Phoebe preaching in any congregation of Christ would have been a violation of God's law.

Junia

However, there is another individual that is often talked about in Romans 16 as well. This individual's name is Junias, believed by some to be the first female apostle, seen in Romans 16:7 KJV:

"Salute Andronicus and Junia, my kinsmen, and my fellowprisoners, who are of note among the apostles, who also were in Christ before me."

Though the KJV says Junia, the Greek says Junias; the name can be either male or female. As we examine whether or not Junias was an apostle and what many believe to be the first female apostle in this verse, there are two important points that we must address pertaining to this verse in accurately applying scriptural apostleship to an individual. These two points are: who qualified to be an apostle? And the capability of the apostles. We will then discuss exactly what is said of Junias and Andronicus in Romans 16:7.

Who Qualified To Be An Apostle?

As we examine the thought of many who believe Junias was the first mentioned woman apostle, it is important for all to understand who qualified to be an apostle. For this examination, we will begin by referencing a couple of facts based in scripture, found in Acts 2:41-42 and Ephesians 2:19-20. We will then reference scripture that is mentioned in the opening chapter of this book in confirming who was qualified to be an apostle of Jesus Christ. Acts 2:41-42 KJV:

"Then they that gladly received his word were baptized: and the same day there were added unto them about three thousand souls. And they continued stedfastly in the apostles' doctrine and fellowship, and in breaking of bread, and in prayers."

As Peter preached Jesus Christ on the day of Pentecost to the Jews, he made the statement, *"ye have taken and by wicked hands have crucified and slain"* (Acts 2:23 KJV); these men, after hearing Peter speak, were pricked in their hearts. They then made a statement to Peter and the rest of the apostles, asking, *"Men and brethren what shall we do?"* (Acts 2:37). This statement made by these men to Peter and the rest of the apostles further confirms that all the apostles were men; yet this is not the point of emphasis. Peter would then go on to say in Acts 2:38-40 KJV:

"Repent and be baptized every one of you in the name of Jesus Christ for the remission of your sins and ye shall receive the gift of the Holy

Spirit. For the promise is unto you, and to your children, and to all that are afar off, even as many as the Lord our God shall call. And with many other words did he testify and exhort, saying, Save yourselves from this untoward generation."

It is after these statements made by Peter that we see the individuals who gladly received his word take action in being baptized for the remission of sins as Peter said and were added to the Lord's church. The specific point of emphasis is found in verse 42, after being added to the Lord's church; *"they continued stedfastly in the apostles' doctrine."* The Greek word *"Didache"* is our English word "doctrine" and is defined as "teaching, the act of teaching, and instruction." All who were taught by the apostle Peter on Pentecost, before being added to the Lord's church, were to continue in all the apostles' teaching while simultaneously being in the Lord's church. Yet, two teachings that came from the apostle Paul are seen in 1 Timothy 2:11-14 KJV:

"Let the woman learn in silence with all subjection. But I suffer not a woman to teach, nor to usurp authority over the man, but to be in silence. For Adam was first formed, then Eve. And Adam was not deceived, but the woman being deceived was in the transgression."

And 1 Corinthians 14:34 KJV:

"Let your women keep silence in the churches: for it is not permitted unto them to speak; but they are commanded to be under obedience, as also saith the law."

If Junias was a woman whom many believe to be the first woman apostle, that would put God at odds with Himself for giving a woman this authority to publicly teach men while at the same time commanding women not to have this authority in the public teaching of men in the Lord's church, as shown in the above verses. By the simple fact that her teachings would be part of the apostles' doctrine to continue stedfast in, thus publicly teaching men as the apostles on the day of Pentecost taught men, and those added to the Lord's church continued stedfastly in the apostles' doctrine, which the world has published [public] in the scriptures. Furthermore, there are two critical points of understanding to be recognized with the statement *"they continued stedfastly in the apostles' doctrine"* in Acts 2:42.

First, the apostles' doctrine [teaching] was not only taught while the Lord's church was assembled; this is evident by the statement *"they continued stedfastly,"* thus showing there was nothing different in the apostles' teaching from before the recipients on Pentecost were added to the Lord's church to after the recipients on Pentecost were added to the Lord's church; there was no change in the doctrine in which the recipients continued stedfast in, confirming women did not have authority on the day of Pentecost to publicly teach the souls added to the Lord's church by the apostles' doctrine. Therefore, the apostles' doctrine is the teaching used to establish the Lord's church and is the same teaching used to maintain the Lord's church **(wholly applied at all times)**; thus showing by the apostles' doctrine that women being prohibited from maintaining the Lord's church in the public teaching of men could not be used to establish the Lord's church in the public teaching of men because the apostles' doctrine is unaltered. This is evident by three scriptural examples I call to your attention. [a] The fact of God specifically implementing men as apostles to publicly proclaim the gospel, [b] the apostle Peter not only preached to establish the Lord's church, he was also able to publicly maintain the apostles' doctrine in the Lord's church by meeting the qualifications to be an elder (1 Peter 5:1), [c] the apostle Paul preached the apostles' doctrine in the marketplace, also known as the town square, outside the Lord's church in Acts 17:17-31; yet he also preached the apostles' doctrine in the Lord's church on the first day of the week in Acts 20:7. Thereby, showing the same standard of the apostles' doctrine was applied in the same way at all times. The apostles' doctrine was scripturally implemented the same way when leading souls to Christ and was unaltered in maintaining those same souls in Christ (the Lord's church) for salvation. According to the apostles' doctrine seen in 1 Corinthians 14:34 and 1 Timothy 2:11-15, we see through God's implementation of the apostles the prominence of the statement *"as also saith the law"* wholly applied in the unaltered apostles' doctrine with the souls taught and those who obeyed on the day of Pentecost.

By this standard, one who says women can publicly teach men outside the Lord's church assembling equally concedes women can publicly teach men when the Lord's church is assembled because the same doctrine used to establish is used to maintain. One who concedes to this point scripturally finds themselves at odds with God's commands, as God has implemented by example, utilizing men as apostles as earthen vessels.

Second, this fact is further confirmed by the apostle Paul in Ephesians 2:19-20 KJV:

"Now therefore ye are no more strangers and foreigners, but fellowcitizens with the saints, and of the household of God; And are built upon the foundation of the apostles and prophets, Jesus Christ himself being the chief corner stone."

As Paul is writing in the Ephesian epistle about the unity in Christ amongst Jews and Gentiles who obeyed the gospel, he makes the statement that Gentiles who were once strangers to the Jews are now fellow citizens with the saints and are of God's household. The point of emphasis is seen in verse 20; the household of God (the Lord's church) is built on the foundation of the apostles and prophets. In order for the household of God to be built, the foundation must be in existence and in place first, upon which the household of God rests, and the foundation that was first laid is permanent, which means the foundation laid before the household of God is built remains the same after the household of God is built. This is precisely the point Paul was making in 1 Corinthians 3:10-11 KJV:

"According to the grace of God which is given unto me, as a wise masterbuilder, I have laid the foundation, and another buildeth thereon. But let every man take heed how he buildeth thereupon. For other foundation can no man lay than that is laid, which is Jesus Christ."

Paul here makes the statement to *"take heed"* (be careful) how one builds upon the foundation laid because the only foundation to be laid is Jesus Christ. Notice that Paul here interchangeably uses *"buildeth thereupon"* in verse 10 with *"other foundation can no man lay that is laid which is Christ"*; explained by the Greek primary particle *"Gar"* (for) in verse 11. Meaning he doesn't make any difference in the building thereupon with the laid foundation as he equally exchanges the two statements. Thus, showing that the teaching is to remain the same and is active as it is being laid even as it is active in the household of God (the Lord's church).

The gospel of Christ has been active since the resurrection of Christ and the commission given to the apostles, as stated in the gospel accounts of Christ. Specifically, I call your attention to Matthew 28:18-20 KJV:

"And Jesus came and spake unto them, saying, All power is given unto me in heaven and in earth. Go ye therefore, and teach all nations, baptizing them in the name of the Father, and of the Son, and of the Holy Ghost: Teaching them to observe all things whatsoever I have

commanded you: and, lo, I am with you alway, even unto the end of the world. Amen."

As we hold particular emphasis on Junias being the first woman apostle and our core scriptures of 1 Corinthians 14:34 and 1 Timothy 2:8-15, the evidence seen in these scriptural facts further demonstrates that the active commands in the Lord's church remain the same as they are being taught by members of the Lord's church outside the order of worship of the Lord's church. The foundation is the apostles' doctrine [teaching], the gospel of Christ. Paul and the other apostles taught and preached for souls to be added to the household of God [Lord's church]. The teaching, which is the foundation, was in existence before it was laid and was to be the same after the foundation was laid, which is the significance of *"taking heed"* to how one builds on the teaching of Christ. This foundation was laid on Pentecost in Acts 2 by the apostles, specifically Peter, as he preached, and the recipients continued steadfast in it. The foundation was laid by Paul to the Corinthians, as Paul stated in 1 Corinthians 3:10-11, and this is the same foundation of which Paul tells the Ephesians they were built upon.

Additionally, as we continue to look at Ephesians 2:20, not only is the household of God built upon the foundation of the apostles, but it is also equally built on the foundation of the prophets (men), as the prophets are equally connected to the apostles by the conjunction "and." In the Old Testament, the foundation (teaching) was maintained by prophets, which is the proclaiming of the grace that is had in Jesus Christ, while at the same time being implemented by God in specifically selecting men to proclaim this teaching. For example, with the prophet and patriarch Jacob in the patriarchal age in Genesis 49:10 KJV:

"The sceptre shall not depart from Judah, nor a lawgiver from between his feet, until Shiloh come; and unto him shall the gathering

of the people ."

And under the Law of Moses in Psalm 118:22 KJV:
"The stone which the builders refused is become the head stone of the corner."

Thus, the sole choosing and implementation of men by God to proclaim the grace had in Jesus Christ in the Old Testament further confirms that the commandment seen in 1 Timothy 2:11-15 was functioning from the very beginning, preceding the order of New Testament worship, as God used the prophets as earthen vessels to spread and maintain this teaching. We will now reference scripture that is mentioned in the opening chapter of this book to confirm who was qualified to be an apostle of Christ.

In Acts 1:15-26, Judas' office was commanded to be filled, as was prophesied by David in the Old Testament, as referenced in Psalm 69:25 KJV:
"Let their habitation be desolate; and let none dwell in their tents,"

And Psalm 109:8 KJV:
"Let his days be few, and let another take his office."

Why was the command specifically for a man to replace Judas' office as an apostle? Careful consideration of Acts 1:21-22 stresses Divine necessity by the Greek word *"Dei"* (must; necessary), which means a man replacing Judas was required within Divine law, confirmed by Peter in Acts 1:20 KJV:
"For it is written in the book of Psalms, let his habitation be desolate and let no man dwell therein: and his bishoprick let another take."

If the command was for a man in Acts 1:15-26 to publicly proclaim Christ before the establishment of the church and we see that Jesus specifically selected all men to be His apostles in the gospel accounts, then by necessary inference (irresistible truth) the command was for Jesus to select all men to publicly teach the gospel.

Mark 3:14 KJV states:

"And he ordained twelve, that they should be with him, and that he might send them forth to preach. the apostles were to be the public criers (heralds), publish and proclaim openly the gospel."

And Luke 6:13 KJV states:

"And when it was day, he called unto him his disciples: and of them he chose twelve, whom also he named apostles; Simon, (whom he also named Peter,) and Andrew his brother, James and John, Philip and Bartholomew, Matthew and Thomas, James the son of Alphaeus, and Simon called Zelotes, And Judas the brother of James, and Judas Iscariot, which also was the traitor."

What law is Jesus following, which is implied by the force of command used in Acts 1:21-22, which necessarily infers a command for Jesus to select men as shown in these verses; which was enforced before the church, used in the founding of the church, and still exists during the era of the church?

The Capability of The Apostles

As we continue our examination of the thought that many hold, which is that Junias was an apostle who was also a woman in Romans 16:7, I am reminded of the apostle Paul's words to the Corinthians in 1 Corinthians 9:2 KJV:

"If I be not an apostle unto others, yet doubtless I am to you: for the seal of mine apostleship are ye in the Lord."

The apostle Paul says to the Corinthians that they are evidence of the fact that he is an apostle in the Lord; a definitive statement of which the Corinthians know to be true. Paul, in making this statement, is advising all that there is a standard by which all can measure an individual to be a true and definitive apostle of the Lord Jesus Christ; therefore, acknowledging a distinction can be seen to separate a true apostle in the Lord from a false apostle. Whatever that standard was, the Corinthians were able to confirm that Paul met all capabilities of that standard, and they could not deny it. We know from our study of "who qualified to be an apostle" that the Lord specifically selected individuals to lay the foundation of teaching, on which the household of God rests, but how was an individual to know if the person who claimed to be an apostle in their teaching was true? The true apostle of the Lord was capable of doing at least two things which confirmed the teaching message they spoke was definitively coming from God; they were able to perform miracles and lay hands on an individual, thus giving them the ability to perform miracles as well. This is vital information in our examination of further confirming if Junias met the standard of being an apostle. The capability that we will focus on is the laying on of the apostles' hands, which also confirms the ability to perform miracles. I call your attention to Acts 8:18-19 KJV:

"And when Simon saw that through laying on of the apostles' hands the Holy Ghost was given, he offered them money, Saying, Give me also this power, that on whomsoever I lay hands, he may receive the Holy Ghost."

Looking at these two verses in Acts 8, we want to place emphasis on Simon. This individual was a person who, according to Acts 8:9 KJV:
"Used sorcery, and bewitched the people of Samaria, giving out that himself was some great one."

Yet, according to Acts 8:13 KJV:
"Simon himself believed also: and when he was baptized, he continued with Philip, and wondered, beholding the miracles and signs which were done."

The use of two Greek words *"proskartero"* (our English word being "continued") and *"theoreo"* (our English word being "beholding") shows that Simon was diligent and very thorough in watching the miracles performed in his continuing with Philip. As Simon carefully followed Philip with wonder, intensely watching him perform miracles, there is a crucial fact to be recognized. Simon, according to the scriptures we've referenced in Acts 8:18-19, desired to have the power to lay hands on whomever he chose to give them the Holy Spirit, meaning Simon wanted to be able to give one the ability to perform miracles. As scripture states, this ability solely came from the laying on of hands of the apostles, which is why the apostles sent Peter and John in Acts 8:14 KJV:
"Now when the apostles which were at Jerusalem heard that Samaria had received the word of God, they sent unto them Peter and John."

After Simon's request, Peter admonished Simon for his request and, while doing so, made a significant statement about the laying on of hands from the apostles; it is the gift of God. Acts 8:20 KJV:

"But Peter said unto him, Thy money perish with thee, because thou hast thought that the gift of God may be purchased with money."

The laying on of hands from the apostles to receive the Holy Spirit was a miraculous gift strictly given to the apostles of God to definitively verify them as ambassadors of Christ in teaching the gospel of Christ, which came from God the Father. The apostles, in laying hands on an individual, gave that individual the ability to perform a miraculous gift as bestowed on said individual by the apostles. We see further confirmation with the apostle Paul having the authority to lay hands on twelve men in Ephesus after they were baptized, giving them two miraculous gifts: to speak in tongues and to prophesy in Acts 19:5-7 KJV:

"When they heard this, they were baptized in the name of the Lord Jesus. And when Paul had laid his hands upon them, the Holy Ghost came on them; and they spake with tongues, and prophesied. And all the men were about twelve."

Additionally, we pay attention to the fact that there was no delay in the laying on of hands from the apostles Peter and John to their recipients in Samaria after hearing of the word being received there; with no delay from the apostle Paul when he laid hands on the twelve men in Ephesus to receive the Holy Spirit. We now come back to Paul's statement made to the Corinthians in 1 Corinthians 9:2: *"If I be not an apostle unto others, yet doubtless I am to you: for the seal of mine apostleship are ye in the Lord."* Regardless of how many people said that Paul was not an apostle of Jesus Christ, the Corinthians were able to definitively confirm that Paul was a true apostle of Christ by the miracles they were able to perform, as Paul said in the beginning of the 1 Corinthians epistle that he came to them in demonstration of the Spirit and power. 1 Corinthians 2:2-5 KJV:

"For I determined not to know any thing among you, save Jesus Christ, and him crucified. And I was with you in weakness, and in fear, and in much trembling. And my speech and my preaching was not with enticing words of man's wisdom, but in demonstration of the Spirit and of power. That your faith should not stand in the wisdom of men, but in the power of God."

A part of Paul's confirmation as a true apostle of Jesus Christ that the Corinthians could definitively confirm was having the ability to demonstrate (manifest and give proof of) the Spirit. For an apostle, this demonstration of the Spirit included the ability to lay hands on an individual, giving them the ability to perform a miraculous gift. The apostle Paul, in his demonstration of the Spirit among the Corinthians, was strong enough to have their faith stand in the power of God; thus, the miracles they were able to perform by Paul's demonstration of the Spirit confirm the statement Paul makes in 1 Corinthians 9:2 to be true. As an example of the miraculous gifts the Corinthians were able to perform, I call your attention to 1 Corinthians 14:14-19 KJV:

"For if I pray in an tongue, my spirit prayeth, but my understanding is unfruitful. What is it then? I will pray with the spirit, and I will pray with the understanding also: I will sing with the spirit, and I will sing with the understanding also. Else when thou shalt bless with the spirit, how shall he that occupieth the room of the unlearned say Amen at thy giving of thanks, seeing he understandeth not what thou sayest? For thou verily givest thanks well, but the other is not edified. I thank my God, I speak with tongues more than ye all. Yet in the church I had rather speak five words with my understanding, that by my voice I might teach others also, than ten thousand words in an tongue."

One may ask, but what does this have to do with Junias being an apostle in Romans 16:7? Well, according to Romans 1:11, one of the reasons Paul wanted to go to the brethren in Rome was so that he may impart some spiritual gift:

"For I long to see you, that I may impart unto you some spiritual gift, to the end ye may be established."

Seeing that an apostle must lay hands on an individual in order for said individual to have a spiritual gift, if there were apostles already there in Rome, they would be able to impart the spiritual gift themselves, and Paul would not have a longing to do so, because apostles were already there to do what Paul desired to do. If Junias and Andronicus were apostles, they would show a standing not equal to the example of all the apostles, with emphasis on Peter, John, and Paul. Whereas the apostles had an immediate reaction in the laying on of hands to those who received the word as seen in Acts 8:14 in sending the apostles Peter and John and Acts 19:5-6 with Paul; the delay seen in Junias and Andronicus with the laying on of hands to those in Rome who have received the word shows they lacked the ability to lay hands on brethren to impart spiritual gifts. According to Romans 1:11, Paul's longing to see the brethren in Rome reflects an urgent desire, thereby showing an immediate reaction to those in Rome receiving the word. Though Junias and Andronicus are already in Rome, this immediate reaction is void in them while examining the scriptures, thereby showing an inability and standing that is not equal to the apostles in the laying on of hands.

Furthermore, the scriptures reveal a definitive statement regarding the Lord's personal involvement as it pertains to His apostles, which is the fact that **"He chose"** specific individuals to hold the office of an apostle. This is seen in the following three sets of verses: Luke 6:13

KJV:
"And when it was day, he called unto him his disciples: and of them he chose twelve, whom also he named apostles."

Acts 1:23-26 KJV:
"And they appointed two, Joseph called Barsabas, who was surnamed Justus, and Matthias. And they prayed, and said, Thou, Lord, which knowest the hearts of all men, shew whether of these two thou hast chosen, That he may take part of this ministry and apostleship, from which Judas by transgression fell, that he might go to his own place. And they gave forth their lots; and the lot fell upon Matthias; and he was numbered with the eleven apostles."

And with Saul, who became Paul, in Acts 9:15 KJV:
"But the Lord said unto him, Go thy way: for he is a chosen vessel unto me, to bear my name before the Gentiles, and kings, and the children of Israel."

As we look at the capabilities of the apostles, the most important point of consideration is that the apostles had no capability without the Lord personally choosing them to hold that office. The Lord personally chose Peter, Andrew, James, John, Philip, Bartholomew, Matthew, Thomas, James of Alphaeus, Simon, Judas brother of James, and Judas Iscariot. Matthias is only mentioned twice in three verses throughout the entirety of the scriptures; yet, the scriptures reveal that the Lord personally chose him as His apostle equivalent to the eleven apostles before him.

Sometime after Matthias, Paul is on the road to Damascus, and he meets the resurrected Jesus Christ, qualifying him to be, as Jesus said he would be, *"a chosen vessel."* Therefore, Paul is qualified to say in 2

Corinthians 12:11 KJV:

"for in nothing am I behind the chiefest apostles, though I be nothing."

The reason being, he met the same standard of the apostles before him; as Jesus also said of Paul in Acts 9:15 what He said to the first twelve apostles in Matthew 10:18 KJV:

"And ye shall be brought before governors and kings for my sake, for a testimony against them and the Gentiles."

There is a definitive statement made that Jesus personally chose these men as His apostles. Scriptural integrity means **"not to think above that which is written"** (1 Cor. 4:6), and therefore, we recognize that if the statement is not made that the Lord personally chose the individual as He did with the fourteen men He personally chose as His apostles, then we cannot say those individuals are equivalent in holding the office of the fourteen apostles the Lord personally chose; because there is an absence of the definitive statement made that Jesus personally chose them.

Therefore, as it pertains to Junias and Andronicus, in the absence of this definitive statement, scriptural integrity forbids us from calling these individuals apostles equivalent to the fourteen apostles the Lord Himself personally chose.

What is said of Junia and Andronicus in Romans 16:7

Now that we have scripturally established the fact that Junias and Andronicus cannot be classified as one of the fourteen apostles the

Lord personally chose, we plainly see in this verse Paul greeting these individuals whom he acknowledges as his kinsmen, which means they are either fellow Jews with Paul or his relatives. An important point of emphasis is the fact that these individuals were also fellow prisoners with Paul. Our English word "fellow prisoner" is translated from the Greek **"sunaichmalotos,"** and is defined as one who is co-captive and sharing imprisonment with another. This word is used only three times in the entirety of the scriptures, and it is Paul who uses the term each time. We've seen it used here in Romans 16:7; it is also used in Colossians 4:10 KJV:

"Aristarchus my fellowprisoner saluteth you, and Marcus, sister's son to Barnabas, (touching whom ye received commandments: if he come unto you, receive him)."

And in Philemon 1:23 KJV:
"There salute thee Epaphras, my fellowprisoner in Christ Jesus."

Each time Paul mentions "fellow prisoner," it is always preceded by the possessive pronoun "my," which shows a relationship of commonality Paul had in being joined together as a fellow prisoner with these individuals. Whatever reason Paul has in common as a prisoner with these individuals must be shown in the reason Paul himself is a prisoner. The scriptures reveal to us the reason for Paul's imprisonment, as seen in the following three sets of verses; Acts 20:20-23 KJV:

"How I kept back nothing that was profitable unto you, but have shewed you, and have taught you publickly, and from house to house, Testifying both to the Jews, and also to the Greeks, repentance toward God, and faith toward our Lord Jesus Christ. And now, behold, I go bound in the spirit unto Jerusalem, not knowing the things that shall befall me there: save that the Holy Ghost witnesseth in every city, saying that bonds and afflictions abide me."

SCRIPTURALLY CAN WOMEN USE PUBLIC PLATFORMS TO TEACH MEN THE GOSPEL OF CHRIST?

Acts 21:11-14 KJV:

"And when he was come unto us, he took Paul's girdle, and bound his own hands and feet, and said, Thus saith the Holy Ghost, So shall the Jews at Jerusalem bind the man that owneth this girdle, and shall deliver him into the hands of the Gentiles. And when we heard these things, both we, and they of that place, besought him not to go up to Jerusalem. Then Paul answered, What mean ye to weep and to break mine heart? for I am ready not to be bound only, but also to die at Jerusalem for the name of the Lord Jesus. And when he would not be persuaded, we ceased, saying, The will of the Lord be done."

And 2 Timothy 2:8-9 KJV:

"Remember that Jesus Christ of the seed of David was raised from the dead according to my gospel wherein I suffer trouble, as an evil doer, unto bonds; but the word of God is not bound."-

The reason for Paul's imprisonment, as explained by Paul in his letter to Timothy, is because he taught the gospel of Christ. Whether he taught the gospel publicly or from house to house, as he told the elders at Ephesus (Acts 20:20-23), it was something that he was ready to be bound and die for (Acts 21:11-14). This experience of Paul's is reflected in his statement *"my fellowprisoner."* Paul was in possession of an experience as a prisoner that he extended to Aristarchus, Epaphras, Andronicus, and Junian, being able to identify with his experience as a prisoner as well. Thereby, showing that these individuals did just as Paul, in teaching publicly and from house to house, they suffered trouble for the gospel of Christ; thus, they are *"fellowprisoners."* However, as it pertains to Junian in Romans 16:7, as we've covered under the section "who qualified to be an apostle"; scripturally, this individual could not have been a woman while publicly teaching men the gospel of Christ, as it is also the apostles' doctrine, used to establish and maintain the Lord's church, the foundation on which the household of God is built and is to continue stedfast in.

Now that we've scripturally established the fact that Junias and Andronicus, who were *"fellowprisoners"* with Paul, are both males by the Lord's standard in having public authority to teach men, which is evident through their shared experience with Paul; we see Paul mention that these men are of "note" among the apostles. With the additional fact that these men do not meet the scriptural choosing from the Lord Himself to be His apostles; we now look at our English word "note," which is the Greek word **"episemos,"** defined as having a mark on it. It can be used in a good sense or in a bad sense, by the fact of Paul giving a mention to salute these men who were his fellow prisoners; their mark is in a good sense among the apostles. Thus, their stand in the gospel of Christ made them well known by the apostles, showing this is the mark these men had.

3

Galatians 3:28: Ye Are All One in Christ

In seeing the varying discussions that many individuals have concerning the topic of "Can Women Use The Public Platform To Teach Men The Gospel," one of the statements often made in defense of women being able to publicly teach men and lead men is found in the words of the apostle Paul to the Galatians in Galatians 3:28 KJV:

"There is neither Jew nor Greek, there is neither bond nor free, there is neither male nor female: for ye are all one in Christ Jesus."

The argument made using this scripture is that men and women are equal in Christ; therefore, the talents and abilities that God has blessed women with ought not to be shackled or held back by the male counterpart. Additionally, it is argued that some women are more talented than men, and many would say this verse proves that more talented women, and those women who maintain a strong zeal for God, are able to publicly teach and lead men in the gospel, in or outside the church, because God has blessed them with that ability and passion.

To this argument, we say that we approach this statement made by Paul in Galatians 3:28 as we do with the entirety of God's word found in scripture. To rightly divide God's word, our approach always begins with: What is the context in which the statement is made? Does the context reference a preexisting law prior to Christ? Does the conclusion drawn from the statement made in this verse contradict scripture stated elsewhere in God's word? How does God implement what is said in this statement as we look at scripture? (What scriptural examples are there?) We will address these four questions in the order in which they were presented.

What is the context of the statement in Galatians 3:28?

When examining scripture, it is highly important to understand what is being discussed within the context of what is stated in the scripture in question. A failure to do so will lead to an interpretation of the scripture under consideration that is not consistent with the flow of thought within the entirety of the letter, and the conclusion drawn from said interpretation can lead to a contradiction of statements made elsewhere in scripture.

As we look at Galatians chapter 1, after Paul gives the introduction of this epistle to the Galatians, he immediately gets to the heart of the situation at hand with the churches in Galatia, in Galatians 1:6-9 KJV:

"I marvel that ye are so soon removed from him that called you into the grace of Christ unto another gospel which is not another; but there be some that trouble you, and would pervert the gospel of Christ but though we, or an angel from heaven, preach any other gospel unto you than that which we have preached unto you, let him be accursed. As

we said before, so say I now again, if any man preach any other gospel unto you than that ye have received, let him be accursed."

Paul here nails down the problem that was taking place in Galatia, with the urgency of immediately focusing on the issue. Initially, after hearing the gospel of Christ, the Galatians obeyed the gospel, which brought them the grace of Christ. Grace, as mentioned here by Paul, is the Greek term **Charis** and is defined as acceptable, benefit, favor, or gift. What benefits man, makes man acceptable, and gives man favor from Christ according to Paul in Galatians 1:6 is found in the gospel of Christ; this ultimately is Christ's help for man. What the Galatians did, and why Paul marveled, is found in the fact that they were so soon removed from the help of Christ found in the gospel to another teaching that Paul acknowledges is not the gospel of Christ, and there were some who were bringing them trouble and were trying to pervert the gospel of Christ.

The problem here in Galatia was so urgent to what Paul was writing as he addressed this situation that Paul tells them if anyone, or an angel from Heaven, preaches another gospel to you than what was initially preached to you, that person is to be accursed. This means they are to be excommunicated; no affiliation with such a person is to be had when they are removing you from the grace of Christ, trying to pervert the gospel of Christ. Additionally, as we look at the Greek word for gospel, it is **Euaggelion**-and is defined as a good message or good news; the good news of the gospel of Christ is that Christ has brought man salvation. Therefore, those who were perverting the gospel of Christ from which the Galatians were so soon removed were removing themselves from Christ's help, namely salvation. As we go forward in the letter of Galatians, we now know the urgent matter that Paul is addressing is the matter of salvation, but why did Paul make

GALATIANS 3:28: YE ARE ALL ONE IN CHRIST

the statement in Galatians 3:28 *"ye are all one in Christ Jesus"*?

Continuing in Galatians 1, after Paul addresses the most important issue of salvation in the gospel of Christ of which they initially heard, he goes on to make a defense of himself, acknowledging that the gospel he preached was to please God, was revealed to him by God, and that God set him aside for the purpose of being an apostle of Christ in Galatians 1:10-24. What we see in Galatians chapter 2 is Paul speaking to the perversion of the gospel and those who were responsible for that perversion. As we look at Galatians 2:1-5 KJV:

"Then fourteen years after I went up again to Jerusalem with Barnabas, and took Titus with me also. And I went up by revelation, and communicated unto them that gospel which I preach among the Gentiles, but privately to them which were of reputation, lest by any means I should run, or had run, in vain. But neither Titus, who was with me, being a Greek, was compelled to be circumcised: And that because of false brethren unawares brought in, who came in privily to spy out our liberty which we have in Christ Jesus, that they might bring us into bondage: To whom we gave place by subjection, no, not for an hour; that the truth of the gospel might continue with you."

As Paul explains, when he, Barnabas, and Titus went to Jerusalem, Titus was not compelled to be circumcised. The mention of Titus's non-circumcision is significant because circumcision was required under the Law of Moses. Prior to Christ, the Law of Moses (which will be further discussed by Paul in Galatians chapter 3) was the law that God gave to Israel as His chosen nation among all nations. Anyone desiring to obey God who was not following the Law of Moses was considered a Gentile; thus, this lets us know that Titus was a Gentile who obeyed the gospel of Christ. This is important information because circumcision is not required in the gospel of Christ, but we see false brethren who came in unaware, spied out the liberty we have in Christ, so they might bring them into bondage; to which Paul did not submit, that the truth of the gospel might continue. The truth of the gospel, once obeyed (Galatians 5:7), is what gives man salvation; to require circumcision to be saved is a perversion of the gospel.

Looking further into Galatians chapter 2:11-21, Paul addresses the problem that was occurring. The Jews who had apparently obeyed the gospel of Christ and were circumcised according to the Law of Moses had a problem accepting the Gentiles as their brethren, (whom God accepts now solely through the gospel of Christ), because the Law of Moses was not being followed by these Gentiles. The Jews separating from the Gentiles was a sinful action by the Jews, an action stating that the Gentiles were not saved. This problem had grown to the point that Paul had to withstand Peter to his face in front of all, Galatians 2:11-14 KJV:

"But when Peter was come to Antioch, I withstood him to the face, because he was to be blamed. For before that certain came from James, he did eat with the Gentiles: but when they were come, he withdrew and separated himself, fearing them which were of the circumcision. And the other Jews dissembled likewise with him; insomuch that Barnabas also was carried away with their dissimulation. But when I saw that they walked not uprightly according to the truth of the gospel, I said unto Peter before them all, If thou, being a Jew, livest after the manner of Gentiles, and not as do the Jews, why compellest thou the Gentiles to live as do the Jews?"

By the standard of Peter's own actions, he did not have salvation and condemned himself by his separation from the Gentiles because they were not living as Jews under the Law of Moses; Peter, who himself was a Jew according to the flesh, was living as a Gentile, meaning he was not applying the Law of Moses to his life for salvation. This is why Paul would go on further to say in Galatians 2:15-21 KJV:

"We who are Jews by nature, and not sinners of the Gentiles, knowing that a man is not justified by the works of the law, but by the faith of Jesus Christ, even we have believed in Jesus Christ, that we might be justified by the faith of Christ, and not by the works of the law: for by the works of the law shall no flesh be justified. But if, while we seek to be justified by Christ, we ourselves also are found sinners, is therefore Christ the minister of sin? God forbid. For if I build again the things which I destroyed, I make myself a transgressor. For I through the law am dead to the law, that I might live unto God. I am crucified with Christ: nevertheless I live; yet not I, but Christ liveth in me: and the life which I now live in the flesh I live by the faith of the Son of God, who loved me, and gave himself for me. I do not frustrate the grace of God: for if righteousness come by the law, then Christ is dead in vain."

Paul himself was also a Jew by nature, but he makes it very clear that for a man to be deemed innocent and righteous (the definition for justified, the Greek word "dikaioo") by God is not by the works of the law, but by the faith of Jesus Christ. Peter and the other Jews who were separating themselves from the Gentiles based on the works of the law, thereby ignoring the faith of Jesus Christ, Paul concludes such actions frustrate (reject) the grace of God. The grace of God, which makes one innocent and righteous with God, therefore giving an individual salvation, Paul here plainly says, is by the faith of Jesus Christ.

As we continue to Galatians chapter 3, we will now see Paul discuss the faith in Jesus Christ, the Law of Moses, and the promise made to Abraham. Paul makes very important points concerning the faith of Jesus Christ of which he just spoke in Galatians chapter 2. We immediately see these important points in Galatians 3:1-8 KJV:

"O foolish Galatians, who hath bewitched you, that ye should not obey the truth, before whose eyes Jesus Christ hath been evidently set forth, crucified among you? This only would I learn of you, Received ye the Spirit by the works of the law, or by the hearing of faith? Are ye so foolish? having begun in the Spirit, are ye now made perfect by the flesh? Have ye suffered so many things in vain? if it be yet in vain. He therefore that ministereth to you the Spirit, and worketh miracles among you, doeth he it by the works of the law, or by the hearing of faith? Even as Abraham believed God, and it was accounted to him for righteousness. Know ye therefore that they which are of faith, the same are the children of Abraham. And the scripture, foreseeing that God would justify the heathen through faith, preached before the gospel unto Abraham, saying, In thee shall all nations be blessed."

The first observation made with these verses is found in the question presented by Paul in verse 2. This question posed by Paul at the beginning of this chapter is the foundation for the statements made and the answer given by Paul in the conclusion of Galatians chapter 3, namely *"Ye are all one in Christ Jesus."* The reason Galatians 3:2 is important as it pertains to Galatians 3:28 is that in Galatians 3:2, Paul is asking a question about salvation. Receiving the Spirit was preached by Peter on the day of Pentecost in Acts 2:38 KJV, as it says:

"Then Peter said unto them, Repent, and be baptized every one of you in the name of Jesus Christ for the remission of sins, and ye shall receive the gift of the Holy Ghost."

Peter told everyone on the day of Pentecost who were pricked in the heart by his preaching of Jesus Christ that they needed to repent and be baptized for the remission of their sins, and they would *"receive the gift of the Holy Spirit."* Then it goes on to say in Acts 2:40-41 KJV:

GALATIANS 3:28: YE ARE ALL ONE IN CHRIST

"And with many other words did he testify and exhort, saying, Save yourselves from this untoward generation. Then they that gladly received his word were baptized: and the same day there were added unto them about three thousand souls."

Notice that Peter said to them *"**Save yourselves from this untoward generation.**"* Three thousand souls on that day took heed to Peter's message of being baptized for the remission of their sins and receiving the gift of the Holy Spirit. Paul in Galatians 3:2 makes the same point to the Galatians that Peter made to those on the day of Pentecost about receiving the Spirit, which leads to salvation; this message comes solely by the hearing of faith in Jesus Christ, as Peter preached the same message on Pentecost. Notice that receiving the Spirit must first come by the hearing of faith, and action is needed for one to be justified by the faith of Jesus Christ (Galatians 2:17), namely being baptized, as Peter says in Acts 2:38, and those who heard him took heed in Acts 2:40-41. Paul also confirms this in Galatians 3:27 KJV:

"For as many of you as have been baptized into Christ have put on Christ."

The works of the law (Law of Moses) lack this message of how to receive the Spirit for salvation and is a law system that required perfect obedience. Those individuals who were trying to pervert the truth of the gospel, as Paul said in Galatians 1:7, were undermining this very critical point for salvation, which is a system inclusive of the Gentiles without having to satisfy the requirements of the works of the law. Paul further confirms this point by asking two more questions that are viewed rhetorically in Galatians 3:3 and 3:5. In verse 3, Paul confirms you received the Spirit by the hearing of faith for salvation, but are you now so foolish as to believe that you are saved by the flesh? (which is the Law of Moses). Furthermore, he confirms in 3:5 that God who gave you the Spirit and worked miracles among you did so by the hearing of faith, which is the preaching of the gospel (Galatians 1:6). This point is extremely powerful because in addition to hearing the gospel, thereby obeying that message of faith which culminated in receiving the Spirit leading to salvation; actual miracles were done among them to confirm the gospel message they were hearing truly came from God. God did not provide this powerful evidence to them by the works of the law.

Next, we see another powerful point in observing Galatians 3:6-9, as Paul tells us it is they that are of faith (established previously as the faith of Jesus Christ) who are the children of Abraham, because those who are of faith believe God as Abraham believed God and are counted righteous in the same way that Abraham was. This was the gospel preached to Abraham well before the Law of Moses was established, **"In thee shall all nations be blessed."** An imperative point for the understanding of all reading this letter to the Galatians, as God preached the gospel to Abraham, He had all nations in mind to be equally called the children of Abraham, before He established the Israel nation and the Law of Moses, of which the Jews, including Peter, were using to separate themselves from the Gentiles, as if they were not saved because of a lack of obedience to the Law of Moses. Paul rightly confirms by scripture that the Gentiles' salvation was well established by God preaching the gospel to Abraham.

From Galatians 3:10-25, Paul further establishes the point that the gospel preached to Abraham is the hearing of faith of Jesus Christ (the gospel—Galatians 1:6) and those individuals who believe are counted righteous just as Abraham, by the fact that Christ was the only man that did through the Law of Moses what no other man could do: deliver us from the curse of the law, which applies to everyone who did not continue in all things which are written in the law to do them (perfect obedience). This gospel preached to Abraham, *"In thee shall all nations be blessed,"* was the promise that God made to Abraham, and God kept that promise as stated in Galatians 3:13-17 KJV:

"Christ hath redeemed us from the curse of the law, being made a curse for us: for it is written, Cursed is every one that hangeth on a tree: that the blessing of Abraham might come on the Gentiles through Jesus Christ; that we might receive the promise of the Spirit through faith. Brethren, I speak after the manner of men; Though it be but a man's covenant, yet if it be confirmed, no man disannulleth, or addeth thereto. Now to Abraham and his seed were the promises made. He saith not, And to seeds, as of many; but as of one, And to thy seed, which is Christ. And this I say, that the covenant, that was confirmed before of God in Christ, the law, which was four hundred and thirty years after, cannot disannul, that it should make the promise of none effect."

Though the Law of Moses came into effect after the promise God made to Abraham, it did not cancel that promise God made to Abraham. Neither was the Law of Moses against the promise God made to Abraham, but the scripture hath concluded all under sin that the promise by faith of Jesus Christ might be given to them that believe. Thus, making the Law of Moses a schoolmaster that led to Christ, so that we might be justified by faith; now that faith has come, we are no longer under a schoolmaster (Galatians 3:21-25). As we have seen from the context of Galatians chapters 1-3, Paul has been discussing issues of salvation; therefore, as we now approach Galatians 3:28, we understand exactly what Paul is talking about, but yet it comes after a specific point that Paul makes in Galatians 3:26-27 KJV:

"For ye are all the children of God by faith in Christ Jesus. For as many of you as have been baptized into Christ have put on Christ."

Close attention to the statements that Paul has made here shows that when one is justified by the faith of Jesus Christ (Galatians 2:16), that individual is known as a child of God. This is how Paul classifies the Galatians, though there were some individuals who were troubling the Galatians and trying to pervert the gospel; prior to this, the Galatians initially obeyed the truth (Galatians 5:7) and by doing this made ***all*** of them ***children of God.*** There is not a single place in the scriptures that reflects any distinction of superiority nor inferiority amongst the children of God when becoming a child of God through Jesus Christ. All children of God receive the same justification by the faith of Jesus Christ. Yet, there are two points of vital importance that must be seen. First, for individuals to be classified as ***children of God,*** according to Galatians 3:27, Paul confirms that said individuals must put on Christ by being baptized. According to Paul, this act of putting on Christ by being baptized is the faith in Christ Jesus, thus being justified by the faith of Jesus Christ. This brings us to our second point; how do we know this statement to be true as seen in Galatians 3:26-27? Because of the word "**For,**" which is the Greek primary particle "***Gar***" that begins both of these verses. This Greek primary particle "***Gar***" properly assigns a reason by explaining what was just stated.

Therefore, we are no longer under a schoolmaster, as stated in Galatians 3:25; the reason for this is explained in Galatians 3:26 by this Greek primary particle "***Gar***" (For), because "***ye are all children of God by faith in Christ Jesus***". The reason for this is explained in Galatians 3:27 by the same Greek primary particle "***Gar***" (For), "***as many of you as have been baptized into Christ have put on Christ.***" All individuals who have taken this action have the same justification by the faith of Jesus Christ with no scriptural distinction of superiority nor inferiority in being a child of God. This is why Paul says in Galatians 3:28 KJV:

"There is neither Jew nor Greek, there is neither bond nor free, there is neither male nor female: for ye are all one in Christ Jesus."

As stated in Galatians 3:16-17, this was the promise that God made to Abraham, thus making those who are justified by the faith of Jesus Christ the seed of Abraham and heirs according to this promise, as stated in Galatians 3:29 KJV:

"And if ye be Christ's, then are ye Abraham's seed, and heirs according to the promise."-

In the epistle of Galatians, as we've seen, the context shows that salvation is the topic at hand; additionally, there is an absence of instruction for the order of worship, authority for teaching, or leading in this epistle, unlike what is seen in 1 Corinthians 14 and 1 Timothy 2. Therefore, to use Galatians 3:28 outside of the context of salvation to try and justify women publicly teaching men the gospel or leading publicly is scripturally erroneous.

Does The Context Reference a Law Prior to Christ?

Paul firmly established that the gospel was preached to Abraham by God in the statement that He made to Abraham *"in thee shall all nations be blessed"* (Galatians 3:8). This statement that God made to Abraham was a covenant and promise, as stated in Galatians 3:16-17 KJV:

"Now to Abraham and his seed were the promises made. He saith not, And to seeds, as of many; but as of one, And to thy seed, which is Christ. And this I say, that the covenant, that was confirmed before of God in Christ, the law, which was four hundred and thirty years after, cannot disannul, that it should make the promise of none effect."

As stated in these verses, this covenant and promise that God made to

Abraham was not disannulled by the Law of Moses, which came after the promise was made by God. Thus, this shows that God is faithful in all His words and holy in all His works, confirming that salvation of being justified by the faith of Jesus Christ was a covenant that was established prior to its fulfillment by Christ and prior to the Law of Moses. Therefore, the statement made in Galatians 3:28 is referencing the preexisting covenant that God made with Abraham (that being equal salvation for Jew and Gentile alike).

Does The Conclusion Drawn Contradict Other Scriptures?

There are two conclusions that we have discussed in our examination of Galatians 3:28. The first conclusion is the idea that women ought to be able to use their talents, abilities, and zeal for God to publicly teach and lead men in the same capacity as their male counterparts based specifically on Galatians 3:28 KJV: **"There is neither Jew nor Greek, there is neither bond nor free, there is neither male nor female: for ye are all one in Christ Jesus."** The second conclusion we've discussed while examining the statements made in Paul's discourse to the Galatians within the context of Galatians chapters 1-3 is that Galatians 3:28 is speaking of salvation; meaning all who desire to be justified by the faith of Jesus Christ are equally the children of God, regardless of race, gender, and social status. We will examine and compare other statements made in scripture as it pertains to these two conclusions to confirm that the conclusions drawn are consistent with rightly dividing the word of God without any contradiction, beginning with the former conclusion.

GALATIANS 3:28: YE ARE ALL ONE IN CHRIST

The thought that women, if they so choose, have the ability to publicly exercise authority over men with teaching or leading in the gospel often comes from one statement in Galatians 3:28 that precedes another statement made in this very verse, and that is *"there is neither male nor female"* which precedes *"for ye are all one in Christ Jesus"*. There are many who believe this gives women God's approval to teach or lead publicly with the gospel on any platform if the desire is there. Yet, we draw attention to another statement made in this very verse and that is *"there is neither bond nor free"*. Therefore, the thought and idea that is being asserted for women based on this verse would be equally true for every group of individuals mentioned in this verse; those in bond (servants) could use their zeal, talent, and abilities for the Lord to free themselves from the restrictions of being a servant to their masters. For us to be consistent with rightly dividing the word of God (2 Timothy 2:15), the conclusion under consideration must apply not only to male and female but also bond and free, Jew and Greek; and there should not be instruction from God on slaves and roles for male and female within His church. Yet, when we examine the gospel, there are several statements made that give instruction to the conduct of slaves and masters, as well as the role of male and female within the Lord's church, and this applies to Jew and Greek because once an individual obeys the truth to be justified by the faith of Jesus Christ, *"ye are all one"*. With regards to those that were known to be bond, I call your attention to two sets of verses, the first being Ephesians 6:5-9 KJV:

"Servants, be obedient to them that are your masters according to the flesh, with fear and trembling, in singleness of your heart, as unto Christ; not with eyeservice, as menpleasers; but as the servants of Christ, doing the will of God from the heart; with good will doing service, as to the Lord, and not to men: knowing that whatsoever good thing any man doeth, the same shall he receive of the Lord, whether

he be bond or free. And ye masters, do the same things unto them, forbearing threatening: knowing that your Master also is in heaven; neither is there respect of persons with him."

The second set of verses I call your attention to is Colossians 3:22-4:1 KJV:

"Servants, obey in all things your masters according to the flesh; not with eyeservice, as menpleasers; but in singleness of heart, fearing God; and whatsoever ye do, do it heartily, as to the Lord, and not unto men; knowing that of the Lord ye shall receive the reward of the inheritance: for ye serve the Lord Christ. But he that doeth wrong shall receive for the wrong which he hath done: and there is no respect of persons. Masters, give unto your servants that which is just and equal; knowing that ye also have a Master in heaven."

In examining both sets of scriptures from Ephesians and Colossians and comparing them with Galatians 3:26-28, all of which were written by Paul, what is scripturally true is that, though these servants were known as *"children of God"*, therefore included in the *"ye are all one in Christ"* seen in Galatians 3:26-28, they were still commanded to be obedient to their masters according to the flesh, and this was the will of God, as seen in the observation of the current sets of verses being examined. It was not the case that the bondservants who were known as being one in Christ no longer had to follow the order of being a servant; however, it was the case that the servant was required to do the will of God within their social position. In like manner, we also see order with the male and female relationship when said individuals are known to be one in Christ. With the male and female relationship in Christ, we see an order, and through God's given instruction, roles were assigned based on the order given. Three sets of verses I call your attention to are scriptures discussed elsewhere in this book, as well as the scriptures that are the core topic of our discussion. First is 1 Corinthians 11:2-3 KJV:

"Now I praise you, brethren, that ye remember me in all things, and keep the ordinances, as I delivered them to you. But I would have you know, that the head of every man is Christ; and the head of the woman is the man; and the head of Christ is God."

The second set of scripture is 1 Corinthians 14:34 KJV:

"Let your women keep silence in the churches: for it is not permitted unto them to speak; but they are commanded to be under obedience as also saith the law."

And the third set of scriptures is 1 Timothy 2:11-15 KJV:

"Let the woman learn in silence with all subjection. But I suffer not a woman to teach, nor to usurp authority over the man, but to be in silence. For Adam was first formed, then Eve. And Adam was not deceived, but the woman being deceived was in the transgression. Notwithstanding she shall be saved in childbearing, if they continue in faith and charity and holiness with sobriety."

With the former conclusion under consideration, drawn from Galatians 3:26-28, in comparison with these sets of scriptures pertaining to the male and female relationship and roles in Christ. After one puts on Christ in Galatians 3:27, we see all are one in Christ from Galatians 3:28; yet, God has given instruction and reason for all to abide by. He set a certain order with roles for man and woman after putting on Christ. One who puts on Christ has confessed to the supreme authority of God over all things, as seen in 1 Corinthians 8:5-6 KJV:

"For though there be that are called gods, whether in heaven or in earth, (as there be gods many, and lords many,) but to us there is but one God, the Father, of whom are all things, and we in him; and one

Lord Jesus Christ, by whom are all things, and we by him."

The one who makes this confession acknowledges God as the source of everything and our Lord Jesus Christ as the agent of creation by whom we have our existence, thus confessing the Godhead's authority over all, with a commitment to abide by God's authority within the instruction that He gives for the entirety of mankind made in His image (Genesis 1:26-27). This authority is not limited to worship service in the Lord's church, but inclusive of it; the reasoning is seen with the context; it goes back to the created order seen in 1 Corinthians 11:8-9 KJV:

"For the man is not of the woman: but the woman of the man. Neither was the man created for the woman; but the woman for the man."

Thus, signifying God's divine order. At the core of 1 Corinthians 11:3-10 and 1 Timothy 2:8-15 is the order of authority founded in the creation order of male and female (which is also the reasoning seen in 1 Corinthians 14:34 *"as also saith the law"*. In all three sets of scripture under examination, the male is the authority because the male was created first, which explains that this order of authority was set in place at the very beginning.

Some would suggest that the reason for Paul's instruction was to acclimate to the social standard of current events within their era and that the Corinthian congregation was severely out of order and this instruction was given as corrective action. However, the reasoning given by God through His apostle Paul explains why God gave this standard, and He does not mention *anything* within the era they were living in as the reason for His order of authority. Additionally, this letter was to be followed by all congregations belonging to the Lord, as Paul addressed all who call on the name of the Lord, along with the Corinthians in the introduction of this letter; 1 Corinthians 1:2 KJV:

GALATIANS 3:28: YE ARE ALL ONE IN CHRIST

"Unto the church of God which is at Corinth, to them that are sanctified in Christ Jesus, called to be saints, with all that in every place call upon the name of Jesus Christ our Lord, both their's and ours"

God's reasoning is based in the creation order of male and female; therefore, transcending the current events of the time these epistles were written, having its origin with Adam and Eve. This standard also applied in the cultural setting of 1 Corinthians 11:3-10 because the order of creation is the reason used in all three settings of 1 Corinthians chapters 11:3-10; 14:34, and 1 Timothy 2:8-15. When an individual desires to put on Christ to become one of God's children, there is an acknowledgment and commitment to follow His instruction and reasoning. Therefore, recognizing God's instruction and reasoning eliminates the female from having the authority to teach men publicly within the Lord's church and publicly outside of the Lord's church.

Furthermore, as we look at 1 Timothy 2:11-15, verse 15 is juxtaposed to verses 11-14. There are three imperative points to understand as this contrast is made in verse 15 from verses 11-14. First, verse 15 begins with the primary particle *"Deh"* used as a conjunction, showing that what is said in verse 15 is equivalent in standard for the female to the standard given for the male in verses 11-14. Verses 11-14 show the reasoning behind the male being given the purpose of authority in teaching men, while in verse 15 there is an equivalent standard, yet a different purpose given for the female, namely the maternal duties had in childbearing.

Second, what is said in verse 15 of the purpose given to the woman is conditioned on a life of faithfulness to the gospel of Christ; therefore, in contrast to the command for women not having authority to teach men, salvation will be had in the purpose of childbearing, guiding and teaching in the role of authority based on the performance of maternal duties. This is seen in the statement made in verse 15 *"shall be saved"*. A life of faith, love, holiness, and sobriety is essential to the gospel of Christ. The conditional particle "if" in this verse lets us know that if the woman is faithful in the gospel of Christ, though she does not have the authority to teach men (as doing so breaks God's command), there is an avenue of authority where she shall be saved, and that is through the performance of maternal duties.

Third, based on the fact that verse 15 is equivalent in standard with verses 11-14 yet has a different purpose than the men, the thought that this set of scriptures solely applies to the worship setting and does not apply outside of worship fails to meet the equivalence of standard seen in the contrast of verse 15 with verses 11-14. In other words, to say that this set of verses only applies to the worship setting and that women may publicly teach men outside of worship would mean the faith, love, holiness, and sobriety required of the woman only applies to the worship setting and is not required outside of worship. This thought, if practiced by the woman, would have one in a state of being double-minded, of which the scriptures tell us is a sin in James 1:8 KJV:

"A double minded man is unstable in all his ways."

And in James 4:8 KJV:

"Draw nigh to God, and he will draw nigh to you. Cleanse your hands, ye sinners; and purify your hearts, ye double minded."

The former conclusion under consideration, the idea that women ought to be able to use their talents, abilities, and zeal for God to publicly teach and lead men in the same capacity as the male counterpart based specifically on Galatians 3:28, has been shown to contradict instruction elsewhere stated within the scriptures with the scriptural examples that we have discussed. Therefore, to come to this conclusion is void of what is stated by the apostle Paul to Timothy in 2 Timothy 2:15 KJV:

"Study to shew thyself approved unto God, a workman that needeth not to be ashamed, rightly dividing the word of truth."

We will now look at the latter conclusion drawn in our discussion of Galatians 3:28; that is, salvation being the topic of discussion based on Paul's discourse within the context of Galatians chapters 1-3. For Galatians 3:28 to convey anything other than salvation, what is said of each class of individuals in this verse pertaining to their oneness in Christ would be conveyed with different reasoning elsewhere in scripture, with each class of individuals being discussed. Yet, that is not what is seen when we look across the scriptures. What is seen is consistent reasoning with the discourse of Paul to the Galatians, with every class of individuals mentioned. We will examine three sets of scriptures confirming this conclusion. As it relates to the classes of race, Jew and Gentile, we highlight Ephesians 2:11-16 KJV:

"Wherefore remember, that ye being in time past Gentiles in the flesh, who are called Uncircumcision by that which is called the Circumcision in the flesh made by hands; that at that time ye were without Christ, being aliens from the commonwealth of Israel, and strangers from the covenants of promise, having no hope, and without God in the world: But now in Christ Jesus ye who sometimes were far off are made nigh by the blood of Christ. For he is our peace, who hath made both one, and hath broken down the middle wall of partition between us; having abolished in his flesh the enmity, even the law of commandments contained in ordinances; for to make in himself of twain one new man, so making peace; and that he might reconcile both unto God in one body by the cross, having slain the enmity thereby."

Paul's reasoning in Ephesians 2:12-16 is consistent with his discourse to the Galatians in chapters 2-3; in particular, Paul says the Gentiles are brought near to God by the blood of Christ; the reason is that Christ, being our peace, has made both Jew and Gentile *one* by breaking down that middle wall of barrier, destroying the law of commandments. This is consistent with why the Jews, including Peter and Barnabas, were separating from the Gentiles and the reason Paul withstood Peter to the face in Galatians 2:11-15.

Prior to Christ, for one to have hope and God, an individual had to be of fleshly Israel, and circumcision was required in the Law of Moses, as seen in Ephesians 2:11-12. That is why there was a compelling by the Jews for the Gentiles to follow this law in Galatians; of which Paul said Titus, who was a Gentile, was not compelled to follow with circumcision (Galatians 2:3) and why Paul withstood Peter to the face for compelling the Gentiles to follow this law (Galatians 2:15).

The Law of Moses was the barrier that brought about opposition from the Jew toward the Gentile in having hope and God, which Jesus destroyed in His flesh, thereby **making in Himself of two, one new man, making peace.** When there was once opposition between Jew and Gentile before Christ; in Christ, Jew and Gentile are one. This is consistent with Galatians 3:26-28 KJV:

"For ye are all the children of God by faith in Christ Jesus. For as many of you as have been baptized into Christ have put on Christ. There is neither Jew nor Greek, there is neither bond nor free, there is neither male nor female: for ye are all one in Christ Jesus."

As it relates to the bond and free, our next example in scripture that we will discuss is seen in Philemon 1:10-16 KJV:

"I beseech thee for my son Onesimus, whom I have begotten in my

bonds: which in time past was to thee unprofitable, but now profitable to thee and to me: whom I have sent again: thou therefore receive him, that is, mine own bowels: whom I would have retained with me, that in thy stead he might have ministered unto me in the bonds of the gospel: but without thy mind would I do nothing; that thy benefit should not be as it were of necessity, but willingly. For perhaps he therefore departed for a season, that thou shouldest receive him for ever; not now as a servant, but above a servant, a brother beloved, specially to me, but how much more unto thee, both in the flesh, and in the Lord."

Paul, in writing to Philemon, who is a free man and master of the servant (a man bond) Onesimus, said there was a time when this servant was unprofitable to Philemon; additionally, Onesimus was a servant that ran away. Paul established a fact about Onesimus's standing as a servant to Philemon as one that was inefficient and detrimental in times past. Given this was Philemon's thoughts towards his servant Onesimus, Philemon, being his master, could have taken measures toward Onesimus for his running away that are not consistent with the gospel of Christ. Though Onesimus was known as unprofitable to Philemon, Paul appeals to Philemon with one statement used two times in verses 12 and 15 *"receive him"*. Onesimus, while with Paul, had obeyed the gospel of Christ; now, instead of viewing him or treating him as unprofitable, he is to be treated by the very definition of his name, profitable. Furthermore, Paul makes a statement in verse 16 of how Philemon is to receive Onesimus, which is also consistent with his statement in Galatians 3:28; Philemon was to receive Onesimus *"not now as a servant, but above a servant, a brother beloved"*. This is consistent with *"there is neither Jew nor Greek, their is neither bond nor free, their is neither male nor female, for ye are all one in Christ Jesus."*

An individual who has chosen to be in Christ Jesus [namely Philemon here] is given instruction in scripture to receive every individual who has made the same choice to be in Christ Jesus (namely Onesimus here) with Godly love as a brother or sister in Christ, regardless of their fleshly social status, race, or gender; because through Christ, all said individuals will have each other forever. Philemon must treat Onesimus more than a servant and no less than a beloved brother to be stedfast in the gospel of Christ. This is why Paul makes the statement of receiving him once again in Philemon 1:17 KJV:

"If thou count me therefore a partner, receive him as myself."

Lastly, as it relates to male and female, our next example in scripture that we will discuss is 1 Peter 3:1-7 KJV:

"Likewise, ye wives, be in subjection to your own husbands; that, if any obey not the word, they also may without the word be won by the conversation of the wives; while they behold your chaste conversation coupled with fear. Whose adorning let it not be that outward adorning of plaiting the hair, and of wearing of gold, or of putting on of apparel; but let it be the hidden man of the heart, in that which is not corruptible, even the ornament of a meek and quiet spirit, which is in the sight of God of great price. For after this manner in the old time the holy women also, who trusted in God, adorned themselves, being in subjection unto their own husbands: Even as Sara obeyed Abraham, calling him lord: whose daughters ye are, as long as ye do well, and are not afraid with any amazement. Likewise, ye husbands, dwell with them according to knowledge, giving honour unto the wife, as unto the weaker vessel, and as being heirs together of the grace of life; that your prayers be not hindered."

The instructions given to the husband and wife through the apostle Peter are consistent with the roles of authority for male and female discussed by Paul in 1 Corinthians 11:3-10; 14:34 and 1 Timothy 2:8-15. Additionally, Paul also discussed the instructions given to husband and wife in Ephesians 5:22-23 KJV:

"Wives submit unto your own husbands as unto the Lord. For the husband is the head of the wife even as Christ is the head of the church: and He is the saviour of the body."

Furthermore, as it pertains to the subjection discussed by Peter in 1 Peter 3:1 and Paul in Ephesians 5:22, it is the same Greek word *"Hupotassō"*-that Paul uses in 1 Corinthians 14:34, as he explains the reason for the subjection of women in the churches is *"as also saith the law."* Yet, careful attention is specifically given to the statement made by Peter in 1 Peter 3:7, *"being heirs together of the grace of life."* Though the role and authority of husband and wife; male and female have a God-given order to them, there is an equal sharing of the same position as heirs of the grace of life. This statement of being heirs together; the Greek word *"Sugklēronomos"* is only used three other times in the New Testament, Romans 8:17 KJV:

"And if children, then heirs; heirs of God, and joint-heirs with Christ; if so be that we suffer with him, that we may be also glorified together."

Ephesians 3:6 KJV:
"That the Gentiles should be fellowheirs, and of the same body, and partakers of his promise in Christ by the gospel."

And Hebrews 11:9 KJV:
"By faith he sojourned in the land of promise, as in a strange country, dwelling in tabernacles with Isaac and Jacob, the heirs with him of the same promise."

Inclusive of 1 Peter 3:7, each time this word is used, it refers to the promise had in Christ, which is salvation. The grace of life is equally given to those individuals who choose to submit to the authority and standard of God, which He supplies through the instruction of His word. The roles for man and woman are different yet followed even by holy women of old time, such as Sarah; but the promise of the grace of life is equally the same for all who choose to be in Christ. Consistent with Paul's statement in Galatians 3:28 KJV:

"There is neither Jew nor Greek, there is neither bond nor free, there is neither male nor female: for ye are all one in Christ Jesus."

How Does God Implement Galatians 3:28?

One of the two conclusions under consideration pertaining to Galatians 3:28 shows intention from the mind of God. In the scriptural examples that we've examined, that conclusion showing the intent of God's mind is salvation. When an individual makes the decision to put on Christ upon being baptized, God, through His inspired apostle Paul, says that all such individuals have equal salvation, are to be treated with the same brotherly love in Christ, and all are equally heirs to the grace of life, regardless of race, fleshly social status, or gender (Galatians 3:28). This intention from the mind of God reveals the will of God for all of man through the redemptive plan of God found only in Christ. Therefore, with the consistency of the scriptural examples that we've examined giving the same reasoning as Galatians 3:28, the instructions seen are how we are to treat each individual upon putting on Christ. Thus, voiding the conclusion of the idea that women ought to be able to use their talents, abilities, and zeal for God to publicly teach and lead men in the same capacity as their male counterparts; to reach this conclusion from Galatians 3:28 shows a contradiction in the intent of the mind of God for the oneness implemented in this verse and is scripturally void of Paul's statement to Timothy in 2 Timothy 2:15 KJV:

"Study to shew thyself approved unto God, a workman that needeth not to be ashamed, rightly dividing the word of truth."

4

Company of Prophets/Sons of The Prophets

As we continue to look at 1 Corinthians 14:34 KJV:

"Let your women keep silence in the churches: for it is not permitted unto them to speak; but they are commanded to be under obedience, as also saith the law."

And 1 Timothy 2:11-15 KJV:

"Let the woman learn in silence with all subjection. But I suffer not a woman to teach, nor to usurp authority over the man, but to be in silence. For Adam was first formed, then Eve. And Adam was not deceived, but the woman being deceived was in the transgression. Notwithstanding she shall be saved in childbearing, if they continue in faith and charity and holiness with sobriety."

In its public application, we continue to see that this law is unaltered in its implementation by God throughout man's history, from the point in Genesis of God creating Adam first to when He initially made the statement to Eve in Genesis 3:16 KJV:

COMPANY OF PROPHETS/SONS OF THE PROPHETS

"And thy desire shall be to thy husband, and he shall rule over thee."

The one place where we see a clear example of public implementation is found with organized groups of prophets, scripturally named the company of prophets, who were likely trained in what is often thought of as the School of Prophets and the scriptural name of the Sons of the Prophets. These individuals, along with prophets such as Amos, who was not affiliated with the organized groups of prophets nor the sons of the prophets, but made a prophet by God under the Law of Moses, show an important fact that is to be recognized. In discussing these prophets within the Old Testament, there is a specific mention of prophet and not prophetess. The word "prophet," which is the Hebrew word ***nâbîy***, is defined as an inspired man who is a spokesperson for the Lord; while "prophetess" is the Hebrew word "***nebîy'âh***" and is defined as an inspired woman. There is not a single place in the scriptures where the Hebrew word ***nâbîy*** (prophet) is directly assigned to a woman. Every time an inspired woman is discussed in the scriptures, the Hebrew word "***nebîy'âh***" (prophetess) is always assigned to her. Thus, when we see the Hebrew word ***nâbîy*** (prophet) used in the Old Testament, we are alerted to the fact that an inspired man is being talked about.

The scriptures speak of the Company of Prophets and Sons of the Prophets in 1 Samuel, 1 Kings, and 2 Kings; however, prior to this time in Israel's history, during the period when Israel was led by judges, before Israel had their first king, a thus saith the Lord was barely given to prophets in Israel. In 1 Samuel 3:1 KJV:

"And the child Samuel ministered unto the Lord before Eli. And the word of the Lord was precious in those days; there was no open vision."

The word was precious in those days, meaning that God very seldom spoke directly to anyone in Israel. Previously, in the book of Judges, we see God only speaking by two individuals, one known by the Hebrew word *"nebîy'âh,"* which is defined as an inspired woman [prophetess]; namely Deborah, as seen in Judges 4:4 KJV:

"And Deborah, a prophetess, the wife of Lapidoth, she judged Israel at that time."

And the other individual who is not named but is known by the Hebrew word ***nâbîy*** (male prophet) in Judges 6:8 KJV:

"That the Lord sent a prophet unto the children of Israel, which said unto them, Thus saith the Lord God of Israel, I brought you up from Egypt, and brought you forth out of the house of bondage."

The differences between the prophetess Deborah and this male prophet are detailed under the section of Deborah, yet I call your attention to the contrast seen in the public prophesying of the male prophet when he speaks what thus saith the Lord to the children of Israel in Judges 6:8, with the person-to-person prophesying that Deborah did when she spoke to Barak, telling him what God had commanded him to do. We do not see another prophet after this time in Judges until the time of Samuel when a man of God came to the priest Eli and spoke what thus saith the Lord to him in 1 Samuel 2:27 KJV:

"And there came a man of God unto Eli, and said unto him, Thus saith the Lord, Did I plainly appear unto the house of thy father, when they were in Egypt in Pharaoh's house"

After this point, we now see God speaking to Samuel in 1 Samuel 3, and Israel recognizing that Samuel was a prophet of God in 1 Samuel 3:20 KJV:

"And all Israel from Dan even to Beersheba knew that Samuel was established a prophet of the Lord."

COMPANY OF PROPHETS/SONS OF THE PROPHETS

From this point, the Lord appeared to Samuel in Shiloh by the word of the Lord, and the word of Samuel came to all Israel, 1 Samuel 3:21-4:1 KJV:

"And the Lord appeared again in Shiloh: for the Lord revealed himself to Samuel in Shiloh by the word of the Lord. And the word of Samuel came to all Israel. Now Israel went out against the Philistines to battle, and pitched beside Ebenezer: and the Philistines pitched in Aphek."

Considering these facts as they pertain to God's seldom speaking to anyone in Israel, we see that once Samuel was chosen and recognized as a prophet of God in Israel, there is mention of more prophets after Samuel, beginning with Samuel anointing Saul as king and the instructions given to Saul in 1 Samuel 10:5, 10 KJV:

"After that thou shalt come to the hill of God, where is the garrison of the Philistines: and it shall come to pass, when thou art come thither to the city, that thou shalt meet a company of prophets coming down from the high place with a psaltery, and a tabret, and a pipe, and a harp, before them; and they shall prophesy."

And verse 10 KJV:

"And when they came thither to the hill, behold, a company of prophets met him; and the Spirit of God came upon him, and he prophesied among them."

Two things that are seen in these verses that have been consistent with God's implementation of what we acknowledge as the authority/subjection law from the beginning in Genesis: first, the company of prophets are male; this we know by the use of the Hebrew word **nâbîy**, which classifies them as men. Second, these men are prophesying publicly. There is a company of prophets publicly prophesying coming down from the high place in verse 5; and when Saul came to the hill in verse 10, there were prophets publicly prophesying there as well, and Saul himself begins to prophesy with this company of prophets, as the scriptures go on to reveal in 1 Samuel 10:11 KJV:

"And it came to pass, when all that knew him beforetime saw that, behold, he prophesied among the prophets, then the people said one to another, What is this that is come unto the son of Kish? Is Saul also among the prophets?"

As we consider these facts, there are three important sets of scripture that are seen within the New Testament that reveal what these prophets in the Old Testament proclaimed. The first two sets of scriptures are seen in Acts 3:18 KJV:

"But those things, which God before had shewed by the mouth of all his prophets, that Christ should suffer, he hath so fulfilled."

And Acts 3:20-24 KJV:

"And he shall send Jesus Christ, which before was preached unto you: whom the heaven must receive until the times of restitution of all things, which God hath spoken by the mouth of all his holy prophets since the world began. For Moses truly said unto the fathers, A prophet shall the Lord your God raise up unto you of your brethren, like unto me; him shall ye hear in all things whatsoever he shall say unto you. And it shall come to pass, that every soul, which will not hear that prophet, shall be destroyed from among the people. Yea, and all the prophets from Samuel and those that follow after, as many as have spoken, have likewise foretold of these days."

In Acts 3, as Peter is preaching to the Jews in the temple in the portico of Solomon, he makes a statement in verse 18 that God showed by the mouth of all the prophets that Christ should suffer. It is important to note the term "all" is inclusive of every single prophet from the very beginning; thus, including Abel and Enoch in Genesis, whom the scriptures call prophets (Luke 11:49-51; Jude 1:14). All who prophesied in the book of Genesis were men. Additionally, as we look at verses 20-24 in Acts 3, Peter mentions that all the prophets from Samuel and those that followed after him proclaimed the days of Christ; therefore, we factually conclude according to the scriptures that these men in 1 Samuel 10 who are publicly prophesying, along with all the prophets after Samuel, have publicly proclaimed Christ. I also call your attention to Ephesians 2:19-20 KJV:

"Now therefore ye are no more strangers and foreigners, but fellowcitizens with the saints, and of the household of God; and are built upon the foundation of the apostles and prophets, Jesus Christ himself being the chief corner."

The foundation on which the church is built is not only the apostles' doctrine; the household of God is equally built on the foundation of the teachings of the prophets. As the scriptures reveal in 1 Corinthians 14:34 and 1 Timothy 2:11-15, women are to keep silence in the churches and not teach nor have authority over men, which prevents women from being apostles, as the church is to continue steadfast in the apostles' doctrine (teaching) as seen in Acts 2:42. This would have women teaching and having authority over men, which confirms the full scope of public teaching; scripturally, we must only teach the apostles' doctrine. The church, equally built on the foundation of the teachings of the prophets, scripturally confirms God, who has spoken by the mouth of all His holy prophets to proclaim Christ, were men; otherwise, the foundation on which the church is built would include women who were prophets teaching the household of God. This is a violation of what is seen in 1 Corinthians 14:34 and 1 Timothy 2:11-15. Yet, we must acknowledge the importance revealed in God's decision to implement men for public authority to teach, which is based on God's commitment to His word that He has given man, thereby showing the importance of Paul's statement *"as also saith the law."*

As we continue to see in 1 Samuel 10:5-11, the scope of influence seen with the prophets of the Old Testament shows the authority the prophets had from God as His spokesmen. With the company of prophets in Gibeah, it is thought that a school of prophets was located in this area. What is to be immediately recognized is that these prophets, through whom God spoke, had a normal habit of utilizing public platforms in the prophesying of God's word, as what is said in these verses shows regular behavior of the prophets already in existence that Saul was going to encounter. Thereby, this further confirms a standard in place for the prophet, without mention of the prophetess. This is evident by the fact that they were prophesying coming down from the high place and the recognition of all who knew Saul before; seeing him prophesy and asking *"Is Saul also among the prophets?"* (1 Samuel 10:11). We also see the company of prophets mentioned in 1 Samuel 19:18-24 KJV:

"And it was told Saul, saying, Behold, David is at Naioth in Ramah. And Saul sent messengers to take David: and when they saw the company of the prophets prophesying, and Samuel standing as appointed over them, the Spirit of God was upon the messengers of Saul, and they also prophesied. And when it was told Saul, he sent other messengers, and they prophesied likewise. And Saul sent messengers again the third time, and they prophesied also. Then went he also to Ramah, and came to a great well that is in Sechu: and he asked and said, Where are Samuel and David? And one said, Behold, they be at Naioth in Ramah. And he went thither to Naioth in Ramah: and the Spirit of God was upon him also, and he went on, and prophesied, until he came to Naioth in Ramah. And he stripped off his clothes also, and prophesied before Samuel in like manner, and lay down naked all

that day and all that night. Wherefore they say, Is Saul also among the prophets?"

In this set of verses, as Saul is sending messengers to take David, we see that Samuel and David dwelt at *"Naioth."* The Hebrew word is translated as *"Targum,"* which is defined as a house of study; also known as a dwelling place for prophets in the time of Samuel. An important point of recognition is that this place was already established, and it was specifically for the prophets, which is further confirmed by verse 20 showing that as the messengers of Saul arrived to take David at Naioth, the company of prophets were there and Samuel standing appointed over them. What is definitive about this set of verses is the fact that it is aligned with what we have recognized about the prophets following Samuel in Acts 3:24 KJV: *"all the prophets from Samuel and those that follow after, as many as have spoken, have likewise foretold of these days."* The church, being the household of God, is built on the foundation of the *"apostles and prophets"* in Ephesians 2:20. The fact that there was a house of study specifically for the prophets, who publicly proclaimed about the days of Christ, of which the church is built on this teaching, and that women are not to teach nor have authority over men further confirms that *"Naioth"* was a house of study and dwelling place specifically for the **nâbîy** (male prophets).

Additionally, we continue to see the same standard applied as we look at the sons of the prophets. "Sons of the prophets" is a technical term, meaning there are specific requirements necessary to meet the standard of being known as one of the sons of the prophets. The term "sons of the prophets" does not mean that they were literal sons and the prophets being the literal fathers, but in reference to the prophets being known as students or disciples of the prophets. The primary requirement is evident in the name "son"; the Hebrew word *"bên"* means a son or male child; thus, one must be male. Each individual male was to study at the feet of the prophet for leadership, instruction of the law, and worship practices, to help preserve the faith of Israel by instructing the nation to return to the righteous ways of the Lord. There are four sets of verses that I call your attention to as we discuss the sons of the prophets, beginning with 2 Kings 2:3 KJV:

"And the sons of the prophets that were at Bethel came forth to Elisha, and said unto him, Knowest thou that the LORD will take away thy master from thy head to day? And he said, Yea, I know it; hold ye your peace."

And 2 Kings 2:5 KJV:

"And the sons of the prophets that were at Jericho came to Elisha, and said unto him, Knowest thou that the LORD will take away thy master from thy head to day? And he answered, Yea, I know it; hold ye your peace."

Looking at these two verses, we note that Elisha is asked by the sons of the prophets about his master, Elijah. Elijah was about to be taken up into Heaven; however, before his translation, he visited Bethel and Jericho, two different locations where the sons of the prophets resided, and Elisha followed him. There are two additional points to consider within these verses.

First, a pattern emerges of the sons of the prophets located in various places. Just as we see the company of prophets in Gibeah in 1 Samuel 10:5-11 and Naioth in 1 Samuel 19:18-24, the sons of the prophets follow this pattern as well, indicating the presence of multiple prophets at different locations throughout Israel. The prophets, through whom God spoke, proclaimed not only about the days of Christ but also provided instruction based on the Law of Moses. This established pattern illustrates that all the prophets were called to proclaim the word of God.

The second point of emphasis is the incorporated system that includes the prophets in relation to the Law of Moses. God utilized these men as His spokesmen to admonish and instruct Israel in the Law and to foretell the coming of the Messiah. This demonstrates God's use of prophets independent of the requirements of worship under the Law. The evidence lies in the consistent pattern of various prophets at different locations throughout Israel. The pattern of *"bên"* (sons) of the *nâbîy* (male prophets) under Elijah and Elisha, as seen in 2 Kings 2, parallels the company of prophets under Samuel. The incorporated system seen in the prophets' public roles outside of worship affirms the required authority needed in this scope of teaching God's word, upon which the church is built (Ephesians 2:20).

Thus, this further illustrates the unaltered nature of the Law and God's consistency in implementing it, as outlined through the inspired apostle Paul in 1 Corinthians 14:34 *"as also saith the law"* and fully explained in 1 Timothy 2:11-15. The next two verses I would like to highlight are found in 2 Kings 4:1 KJV:

"Now there cried a certain woman of the wives of the sons of the prophets unto Elisha, saying, Thy servant my husband is dead; and thou knowest that thy servant did fear the LORD: and the creditor is come to take unto him my two sons to be bondmen."

And 2 Kings 6:1-2 KJV:

"And the sons of the prophets said unto Elisha, Behold now, the place where we dwell with thee is too strait for us. Let us go, we pray thee, unto Jordan, and take thence every man a beam, and let us make us a place there, where we may dwell. And he answered, Go ye."

SCRIPTURALLY CAN WOMEN USE PUBLIC PLATFORMS TO TEACH MEN THE GOSPEL OF CHRIST?

In 2 Kings 4:1, the husband of a certain woman, who was one of the sons of the prophets, had died; yet there is a statement that she makes about the life of her husband prior to his death, *"Thy servant did fear the LORD."* This son of the prophets not only served Elisha in this capacity as a prophet, but he also served the Lord as a prophet. This capacity of serving required public proclamation, as Elisha is publicly serving the Lord as a prophet and instructing the sons of the prophets in publicly serving the Lord. With the sons of the prophets, along with the company of prophets, prophesying the word of God (1 Samuel 19:20), being in alignment with the scriptural requirement of these individuals having to be men, as we have discussed; we further confirm scripturally that God has reserved the serving of the prophets in this capacity with all of its functional duties detailed in scripture for males. This continues to be evident by the statements seen in 2 Kings 6:1-2; here it is said that the sons of the prophets dwell with Elisha; yet the term here for dwell is defined in its literal statement of *"the place where we sit in front of you,"* which is equivalent to a classroom. Thus, it shows that the serving the sons of the prophets did under Elisha required instruction, and that instruction was based on the word of God. With the dwelling in 2 Kings 6:1 being too small, the sons of the prophets requested to build a bigger dwelling in which to serve under Elisha as prophets; thereby, serving the Lord.

Additionally, there are three sets of scriptures that I call your attention to as we confirm that the sons of the prophets, in being servants of Elisha, were also servants of the Lord as they functioned in the capacity of a prophet. The first set of scriptures is seen in Amos 3:1-2; 6-9 KJV:

"Hear this word that the Lord hath spoken against you, O children of Israel, against the whole family which I brought up from the land of Egypt, saying, you only have I known of all the families of the earth: therefore I will punish you for all your iniquities."

Amos, as he speaks in the name of the Lord, addresses the sons of Israel and the whole family which the Lord *"brought up from the land of Egypt."* Being the public spokesman on behalf of the Lord, Amos addresses Israel because of their iniquities; this alerts us to the fact that the prophet was allowed by God to speak publicly to the nation regarding the error of their ways, thus the prophet was able to admonish the nation outside of the required worship seen in the Law of Moses. Though Amos did not receive instruction as a son of the prophets, nor was he among the company of prophets; as he says of himself in Amos 7:14 KJV:

"Then answered Amos, and said to Amaziah, I was no prophet, neither was I a prophet's son; but I was an herdman, and a gatherer of sycomore fruit."

He was still chosen by God to prophesy His word, as Amos also says in Amos 7:15 KJV:

"And the LORD took me as I followed the flock, and the LORD said unto me, Go, prophesy unto my people Israel."

Thereby, one who was qualified to function as a prophet had the capacity to publicly admonish Israel for their sins under the Law of Moses, as well as proclaim the days of Christ. Furthermore, I call your attention to Amos 3:6-9 KJV:

"Shall a trumpet be blown in the city, and the people not be afraid? shall there be evil in a city, and the LORD hath not done? Surely the Lord GOD will do nothing, but he revealeth his secret unto his servants the prophets. The lion hath roared, who will not fear? the Lord GOD hath spoken, who can but prophesy? Publish in the palaces at Ashdod, and in the palaces in the land of Egypt, and say, assemble yourselves upon the mountains of Samaria, and behold the great tumults in the midst thereof, and the oppressed in the midst thereof."

As Amos continues to speak in the name of the Lord, he continues to confirm the authority God has given the prophets to publicly speak on His behalf, through the rhetorical questions seen in verse 6, in asking; shall a trumpet be blown in the city and the people not be afraid? Shall there be destruction in a city and the Lord has not done? What is seen in Amos 3:6-8 is the Lord making an equal comparison with the warning signs given to a city about looming destruction through His providential work (verse 6); with the warning signs He has given to His prophets, who are His public servants speaking on His behalf (verses 7-8). The public nature of looming destruction to an entire city not only confirms the scope of influence of the **nâbîy** (male prophets) in verses 7 and 8, but it is also seen in the instruction of verse 9 by God's command to make public the prophecy in the palaces at Ashdod and Egypt.

Furthermore, the phrase *"His servants the prophets"* in Amos 3:7 shows an official designation for this specific service by the Lord. The possessive pronoun "His" confirms that the prophets belonged to the Lord; the arena of use of the prophets by the Lord confirms the purpose the Lord had for these prophets. The course of action laid out in the scriptures confirms the Lord's usage of His prophets to be carried out publicly to the people. The possessiveness of the prophets belonging to the Lord is also seen in the phrase *"My servants the prophets."* These official designations are known to be true in the fact that these phrases of possession are repeated throughout the Old Testament scriptures; for our further examination, we will see this phrase in 2 Kings 17:13 and Daniel 9:9-10.

First, what must be understood about these phrases is the fact that they are used of the prophets immediately following the period of tutelage seen by Samuel, Elijah, and Elisha in 1 Samuel and 1 and 2 Kings. This alerts us to a point of emphasis in the fact that when Samuel was a child, God rarely spoke to the people; as stated in 1 Samuel 3:1 KJV:

"And the word of the LORD was precious in those days there was no open vision."

However, as Samuel becomes of age and is recognized as a prophet of God by *"all Israel from Dan even to Beersheba"* (1 Samuel 3:20), we see him as head over the company of prophets in training them (1 Samuel 19:20). Samuel made every effort to follow the Law of Moses, as he says to Israel, *"God forbid that I should sin against the LORD in ceasing to pray for you: but I will teach you the good and the right way"* (1 Samuel 12:23). As Samuel followed the Law in teaching the company of prophets, of whom God used publicly; it must be acknowledged that Samuel also followed the Law in recognizing that the individuals he taught must have the authority to speak publicly on the Lord's behalf. We see the requirement in the use of the term ***nâbîy*** and in the technical term "sons of the prophets" was officially reserved for males by the Lord to serve in this capacity. Therefore, the official designation of the phrases *"His servants the prophets"* and *"My servants the prophets"* could only be applied to males committed to serving the Lord by His word. Thereby, we see the public areas that God used *"His servants the prophets"* in the Old Testament confirm the statement *"as also saith the law"* (1 Corinthians 14:34) and explained in 1 Timothy 2:11-15 in the New Testament, moved beyond the arena of worship service.

Now, as we examine the Old Testament scriptures of 2 Kings 17:13 and Daniel 9:9-10, we will see one of the core responsibilities required of the prophets from God as He uses the possessive pronouns "My" and "His" in the phrases *"My servants the prophets"* and *"His servants the prophets."* As we realize just what the Law of Moses is to the church, 2 Kings 17:13 KJV:

> *"Yet the LORD testified against Israel, and against Judah, by all the prophets, and by all the seers, saying, Turn ye from your evil ways, and keep my commandments and my statutes, according to all the law which I commanded your fathers, and which I sent to you by my servants the prophets."*

And Daniel 9:9-10 KJV:

> *"To the Lord our God belong mercies and forgivenesses, though we have rebelled against him; Neither have we obeyed the voice of the LORD our God, to walk in his laws, which he set before us by his servants the prophets."*

In looking at 2 Kings 17:13, we first acknowledge the fact that there is a clear distinction made with the usage of the phrase *"**My servants the prophets**"* and the use of the prophets by the Lord in this verse; with 2 Kings 22:14-22 and the usage of the term prophetess to describe Huldah and her usage just five chapters after this verse. More on Huldah the prophetess is discussed in the chapter on Deborah, Huldah, and Priscilla. Furthermore, as we look at 2 Kings 17:13 and Daniel 9:9-10, what is evident is the fact that the work of the prophets required them to teach the commandments of the Law of Moses as the prophets admonished Israel to turn away from their sins. This fact is highly important as it pertains to what the entirety of the Law of Moses is to the doctrine of Christ and His church. In confirming what the Law of Moses is to the doctrine of Christ, I call your attention to three sets of verses: Hebrews 5:12 KJV:

> *"For when for the time ye ought to be teachers, ye have need that one teach you again which be the first principles of the oracles of God; and are become such as have need of milk, and not of strong meat."*

Hebrews 6:1-2 KJV:

"Therefore leaving the principles of the doctrine of Christ, let us go on unto perfection; not laying again the foundation of repentance from dead works, and of faith toward God, of the doctrine of baptisms, and of laying on of hands, and of resurrection of the dead, and of eternal judgment."

And Romans 3:21-22 KJV:

"But now the righteousness of God without the law is manifested, being witnessed by the law and the prophets; even the righteousness of God which is by faith of Jesus Christ unto all and upon all them that believe: for there is no difference."

In examining the Hebrew letter, what is highly evident is the comparison and contrast of the Law of Moses with the gospel of Christ, by the superiority of the gospel of Christ over the Law of Moses. Jews by the flesh who obeyed the gospel of Christ were evidently considering leaving the gospel of Christ and going back to living under the Law of Moses. These Jews, after obeying the gospel of Christ, suffered hard struggles, afflictions, and were publicly exposed to reproach and were admonished not to throw away their confidence in Christ; thereby doing the will of God in Christ; they will receive what is promised (Hebrews 10:32-36). The Hebrews writer, through this letter, warns these Jewish Christians of the dangers of leaving Christ, and as we also see in our highlighted verses of Hebrews, taught them that the Law of Moses is the beginning principles of God's word (oracles).

The Hebrews writer had much to say about Jesus being priest after the order of Melchizedek; the oath of Jesus' priesthood being after the order of Melchizedek is solely found in the Law of Moses (Psalm 110:4). Yet, the Jewish Christians whom the Hebrews writer is speaking to did not understand the Law of Moses and needed to be taught the Law of

Moses again, as he realizes they are in need of milk (teaching in the Law of Moses) and are unskillful in the word of righteousness; that being the gospel of Christ (**also seen in Romans 3:21-22**). Here we see an important fact about the Law of Moses as it pertains to Christ; that being, it was the standard of teaching concerning the Messiah prior to its fulfillment in the Messiah. Scripturally, in the apostles' doctrine, this is how the Law of Moses is to be taught and viewed, and this is exactly how it is presented here in Hebrews, which is the apostles' doctrine and is also the gospel of Christ given by inspiration of God. A fact that is to be acknowledged with this information is that the Law of Moses, being the standard of teaching about Christ prior to its fulfillment in Christ, is to be presented as such in the apostles' doctrine. This means those who lived under the Law of Moses could not have women publicly teaching the law because of its presentation in the apostles' doctrine. This is why we see God tell the prophet Moses in Deuteronomy 5:31 KJV:

"But as for thee, stand thou here by me, and I will speak unto thee all the commandments, and the statutes, and the judgments, which thou shalt teach them, that they may do in the land which I give them to possess it."

And why God uses His servants the *nâbîy* (male prophets) specifically as His public spokesmen; the Law of Moses was the beginning foundation of teaching for the Lord's church.

Furthermore, this is also evident in what is seen in Hebrews 6:1 as the Hebrews writer says to **leave** the beginning teachings of Christ. The desire to go back to live under the Law of Moses was a desire to live on milk as a babe does; however, the time had come through Christ's fulfillment of the Law of Moses to move beyond the stage of milk to solid food for the mature; that being the word of righteousness which is the gospel of Christ. Notice in this verse the Hebrews writer says **"not laying again a foundation of repentance from dead works and faith toward God;"** the prophet Moses and all God's prophets had already laid the foundation of repentance from dead works and faith toward God. This much is seen in 2 Kings 17:13, where it is said by God through His servants the prophets:

"Turn ye from your evil ways, and keep my commandments and my statutes, according to all the law which I commanded your fathers"

And in Daniel 9:10, where the prophet Daniel writes:

"Neither have we obeyed the voice of the LORD our God, to walk in his laws, which he set before us by his servants the prophets."

Additionally, the foundation was already laid in the Law of Moses with the teaching of washings, laying on of hands, resurrection of the dead, and eternal judgment. The teaching of washings in the Law of Moses is also discussed in Hebrews 9:8-10 KJV:

"The Holy Ghost this signifying, that the way into the holiest of all was not yet made manifest, while as the first tabernacle was yet standing; which was a figure for the time then present, in which were offered both gifts and sacrifices, that could not make him that did the service perfect, as pertaining to the conscience; which stood only in meats and drinks, and divers washings, and carnal ordinances, imposed on them until the time of reformation."

(The same plural word for washings **baptismos** in Hebrews 6:1 is also used in Hebrews 9:10). The teaching of the laying on of hands discusses the transferring of one's sins to their sacrificial offering as seen in Leviticus 3:8 KJV:

"And he shall lay his hand upon the head of his offering and kill it before the tabernacle of the congregation: and Aaron's sons shall

sprinkle the blood thereof round about upon the altar."

The teaching of the resurrection from the dead and eternal judgment are seen in Daniel 12:2 KJV:

"And many of them that sleep in the dust of the earth shall awake, some to everlasting life, and some to shame and everlasting contempt."

And Ecclesiastes 12:14 KJV:

"For God shall bring every work into judgment, with every secret thing, whether it be good, or whether it be evil."

Thus, the foundation of Christian teaching stems from this earlier teaching in the Law of Moses, finding its fulfillment in Christ; of which we remind you, the apostle Paul says in Ephesians 2:20 KJV:

"And are built upon the foundation of the apostles and prophets, Jesus Christ himself being the chief corner."

The apostles' doctrine emphasizes the fact that the Law of Moses and the prophets are fulfilled in Christ. Thus, the doctrine of the apostles stems from the beginning teachings of Christ, which is the Law of Moses. The church is built on the fact that the beginning teaching of Christ is fulfilled in Christ, which the apostles' doctrine affirms. There, therefore, is an equivalent standard with all who publicly taught the Law of Moses in the Old Testament with all the apostles of Christ in the New Testament. The standard of law forbidding women to be apostles by the apostles' doctrine, in the fact that the church must continue steadfast in the apostles' doctrine, is equally found in the Law of Moses given to the prophet Moses for all of physical Israel to obey. As the foundation that the church is built on is the apostles and prophets.

Therefore, the doctrine the apostles taught on the day of Pentecost; of which the church must continue steadfast in after obedience to it (Acts 2:42); forbade women to be apostles of Christ, by the fact they were unable to maintain the role of publicly teaching the Lord's church (1 Corinthians 14:34 and 1 Timothy 2:11-1) stems from those who taught the beginning teachings of Christ (Law of Moses) to all of physical Israel. Scripturally, this information affirms the fact beyond any doubt; those who publicly taught the Law of Moses were required to be a male prophet (***nâbîy***), as the church is built on those who publicly taught it. Thus, those prophets are teaching the church through scripture which is given by inspiration of God (2 Timothy 3:16-17).

5

The Prophetesses of Scripture

Thus far in the Scriptures, we've examined God implementing His standard for how public teaching of His word is to be done with His approval, and we've seen consistently from Genesis throughout the Scriptures that it is the male whom God has specifically and intentionally chosen for this function. However, this does not negate the scriptural evidence that God has also used women to speak on His behalf with His approval, and the women whom God chose were known as Prophetesses. Yet there is a standard that God says we are not to violate, which is based on the statement that the Apostle Paul made in 1 Corinthians 14:34 ***"as also saith the law,"*** and as we've been discussing within this book, this statement is further explained in 1 Timothy 2:8-15. With this in mind, we must ask important questions to gain critical and necessary information that we must rightly extract from the Scriptures concerning how God implemented the women He chose to be Prophetesses, and they are as follows: How did God implement the women Prophetesses?

Was God's use and implementation of the Prophetess on equal ground with God's use of the male prophets? As Paul stated in the Gospel of Christ, the law is from the beginning, and God does not break His law. This is recorded for us in Scripture with one example seen in Romans 3:4 KJV:

"God forbid: yea, let God be true, but every man a liar; as it is written, that thou mightest be justified in thy sayings, and mightest overcome when thou art judged."

In light of the scriptural implementation of the authority/subjection law the Scriptures have laid out, we can draw one of two conclusions: either God broke His law, which would make Him a liar—this is incorrect because Scripture tells us in Hebrews 6:18 KJV: *"It is impossible for God to lie,"*—or there was another avenue that God used to implement the women Prophetesses in Scripture. As we examine the two questions posed in this section pertaining to the Prophetesses, we will discuss each one in order from the Scriptures as they appear, with the first one being Miriam.

Miriam

Miriam, the sister of Moses, most likely first appears in scripture not by name, as she watches her brother Moses float down the Nile River before he is taken up by Pharaoh's daughter, as recorded in Exodus 2:3-4 KJV:

"And when she could not longer hide him, she took for him an ark of bulrushes, and daubed it with slime and with pitch, and put the child therein; and she laid it in the flags by the river's brink. And his sister stood afar off, to wit what would be done to him."

However, Miriam is first mentioned by name as the sister of Aaron in Exodus 15:20. Additionally, we know that Miriam is the sister of Moses because scripture confirms that Aaron, Moses, and Miriam had the same mother and father, as recorded in Numbers 26:59 KJV:

"And the name of Amram's wife was Jochebed, the daughter of Levi, whom her mother bare to Levi in Egypt: and she bare unto Amram Aaron and Moses, and Miriam their sister."

I now draw your attention back to the first question posed in this section: How did God implement the women Prophetesses? As we look at Miriam in Exodus 15:20 KJV, God first makes us aware of a Prophetess in His word by Miriam being a Prophetess, as it says:

"And Miriam the prophetess, the sister of Aaron, took a timbrel in her hand; and all the women went out after her with timbrels and with dances."

From this verse, we see a function of what the Prophetess did, which Miriam filled. The Prophetess led all the women of Israel. With over 600,000 Israelites leaving Egypt, as Exodus 12:37 KJV tells us:

"And the children of Israel journeyed from Rameses to Succoth, about six hundred thousand on foot that were men, beside children."

Yet it was all the women that Miriam was tasked to by God. The word that Miriam, being a prophetess, gave to all the women is seen in Exodus 15:21 KJV:

"And Miriam answered them, Sing ye to the Lord, for He hath triumphed gloriously; the horse and his rider hath He thrown into the sea."

The scriptures not condemning Miriam for this role that she is functioning in, with these two verses, confirms that she had God's approval for this task that she was fulfilling, which scripture shows as to the women. The second question that is asked in this section is: Was God's use and implementation of the prophetess on equal ground with God's use of the male prophets? As it pertains to Miriam, I will call our attention to specific details that are seen in the book of Numbers Chapters 12:1-10. Yet, before we discuss this set of scriptures, I would like for us to pay attention to detail as it pertains to Moses, Aaron, and Miriam with three specific verses that mention them together. The first two of these three verses that I call to your attention are Numbers 26:59 KJV:

"And the name of Amram's wife was Jochebed, the daughter of Levi, whom her mother bare to Levi in Egypt: and she bare unto Amram Aaron and Moses, and Miriam their sister."

And 1 Chronicles 6:3 KJV:
"And the children of Amram; Aaron, and Moses, and Miriam. The sons also of Aaron; Nadab, and Abihu, Eleazar, and Ithamar."

I bring your attention to these verses because each time there is a mention of the children of Amram, we see a specific order of Amram's children: first, Aaron; second, Moses; and third, Miriam. Though Miriam was most likely older than Aaron and Moses (as seen in Exodus 2:3-4, which we've listed earlier in this section), Aaron was only three years older than Moses, according to Exodus 7:7 KJV:

"And Moses was fourscore years old, and Aaron fourscore and three years old, when they spake unto Pharaoh."

Aaron, being only three years older than Moses, doesn't give him the mental or physical maturity to report who took Moses at the Nile River, leaving Miriam, who did have that capability and reported to their mother, to be older than Aaron. The reason for Miriam being listed last among the three of Amram's children, though she is the oldest, is that emphasis is placed on the males as the lead. The oldest male takes the lead among the children, which was Aaron; the second oldest male was Moses; and then Miriam, as scripture concludes all of Amram's children with these three. The order given here reflects who took the lead among the children within the family of Amram and Jochebed, which was the males. However, in the third verse that specifically mentions all the children of Amram together, we see a different order, which is the order that God put in place regarding the leadership of the children of Israel. This is seen in Micah 6:2-4 KJV:

"Hear ye, O mountains, the Lord's controversy, and ye strong foundations of the earth: for the Lord hath a controversy with his people, and he will plead with Israel. O my people, what have I done unto thee? and wherein have I wearied thee? testify against me. For I brought thee up out of the land of Egypt and redeemed thee out of the house of servants; and I sent before thee Moses, Aaron, and Miriam."

Emphasis is placed on the order of the three in verse 4 with Moses, Aaron, and Miriam. This is the order that God put in place to lead Israel; it is always Moses first because God chose Moses to lead, then Aaron, and then Miriam. We see this specifically with Moses and Aaron in numerous other verses as well, one of which I've mentioned earlier in this book comes from Psalm 105:26 KJV:

"He sent Moses his servant; and Aaron whom he had chosen."

When it came to God dealing with Israel, He never stepped out of that order. He always began by conveying His word with His chosen leader over all of Israel, which was Moses. I now bring your attention to Numbers chapter 12:1-10, where we see a challenge to the leadership of Moses. We'll examine, first, Numbers 12:1-2 KJV:

"And Miriam and Aaron spake against Moses because of the

Ethiopian woman whom he had married: for he had married an Ethiopian woman. And they said, Hath the Lord indeed spoken only by Moses? hath he not spoken also by us? And the Lord heard it."

Here we see a challenge to Moses' leadership by his very own siblings, Miriam and Aaron. The basis for their challenge to the leadership of Moses was his marriage to the Ethiopian woman. In these two verses, there are four pieces of information that we can take from this set of scriptures. First, we know that Moses was God's leader and public figure for the entire nation of Israel; Moses is who God chose for this function (he is the type to Christ's anti-type). Second, when Miriam and Aaron spoke against Moses because of his marriage to the Ethiopian woman, they were, in essence, saying they could function in the role that was given to Moses as well, or in other words, they could lead Israel just as Moses was doing. Third, we know this to be the case based on what they both said in verse 2, which was *"Hath the Lord indeed spoken only by Moses? hath He not spoken also by us?"* Their position was that they were a prophetess and a prophet too; God gives us His word to convey as well. The fourth and most crucial piece of information in this discussion from these two verses is the order of the names presented among the two in their challenge to Moses' leadership; Miriam is listed first. While both Miriam and Aaron took the initiative upon themselves to break God's order and role He had given them, Miriam took the lead between the two of them in challenging Moses' leadership. We've noted earlier in this section that the role given to Miriam in Exodus 15:20-21 was to all the women.

How do we know that this is the case, that Miriam took the lead between her and Aaron in challenging Moses' leadership? Let's look at the order that God calls them, as we continue to read in Numbers 12:3-5 KJV:

SCRIPTURALLY CAN WOMEN USE PUBLIC PLATFORMS TO TEACH MEN THE GOSPEL OF CHRIST?

"Now the man Moses was very meek, above all the men which were upon the face of the earth. And the Lord spake suddenly unto Moses, and unto Aaron, and unto Miriam, Come out ye three unto the tabernacle of the congregation. And they three came out. And the Lord came down in the pillar of the cloud, and stood in the door of the tabernacle, and called Aaron and Miriam: and they both came forth."

As it pertains to Moses, God, through His word, tells us that Moses was very meek; in other words, he was humble and didn't address the challenge made by Miriam and Aaron. So God spoke suddenly in the order that He initially called the three in the role that He had given them: Moses first, Aaron second, and Miriam third. The order seen in verse 1 tells us who took the lead in the challenge to Moses, and the order in verses 4-5 tells us who has the lead through the approved standard by God. After God called Moses, Aaron, and Miriam in verse 4, we further see the approved standard of order in verse 5, as God now only calls the two who challenged Moses' leadership, yet not in the order we see in verse 1; here God calls Aaron first and Miriam second.

In verses 1-2, Aaron and Miriam both sinned because they challenged God's order in leading Israel. In verse 4, God calls all three of them by the order He implemented for leading Israel. In verse 5, we see a reversal of the order seen in verse 1, with God calling Aaron first and Miriam second, demonstrating that the male, by His standard, is the lead. The significance of the order seen here in verse 5 goes hand in hand with the roles given to Aaron and Miriam. In Aaron's role and function as a prophet, God publicly used Aaron to teach the man who was Pharaoh that he was dealing with God. Through the miracles He worked by the hand of Aaron, God affected all of Egypt, both male and female. One of many examples is seen in Exodus 7:19-21 KJV:

"And the Lord spake unto Moses, Say unto Aaron, Take thy rod, and stretch out thine hand upon the waters of Egypt, upon their streams, upon their rivers, and upon their ponds, and upon all their pools of water, that they may become blood; and that there may be blood throughout all the land of Egypt, both in vessels of wood, and in vessels of stone. And Moses and Aaron did so, as the Lord commanded; and he lifted up the rod, and smote the waters that were in the river, in the sight of Pharaoh, and in the sight of his servants; and all the waters that were in the river were turned to blood and the fish that was in the river died; and the river stank, and the Egyptians could not drink of the water of the river; and there was blood throughout all the land of Egypt."

However, the function given to Miriam was in the role of leading all the women of Israel as a prophetess. From these two distinct roles as prophet and prophetess given to Aaron and Miriam respectively, we see a difference in how God has implemented both. For one, namely Aaron, his role encompassed a public platform affecting all of Egypt, male and female, simultaneously. For Miriam, her role encompassed all the women of Israel, as we've seen in Exodus 15:20-21. While Aaron and Miriam sinned because they both challenged God's order in leading Israel, Miriam also sinned in that she broke God's law discussed by the apostle Paul in 1 Corinthians 14:34 *"as also saith the law"*; this law is further explained in 1 Timothy 2:8-15. This example further shows how God implemented this law throughout history. As we continue to look at Numbers 12, God speaks with Aaron and Miriam, asking why they were not afraid to speak against Moses, the one who was faithful in all His house, with whom God spoke face to face and has even seen the similitude of God. In God's reprimanding of Aaron and Miriam for their desire to take public lead over Moses in all Israel, God is definitively clear on whom He has chosen to lead Israel: that being

Moses, and who He would make Himself known to on a scale lower than Moses in publicly addressing Israel, that being a prophet, not a prophetess, as seen in Numbers 12:6-9 KJV:

"And he said, Hear now my words: If there be a prophet among you, I the Lord will make myself known unto him in a vision, and will speak unto him in a dream. My servant Moses is not so, who is faithful in all mine house. With him will I speak mouth to mouth, even apparently, and not in dark speeches; and the similitude of the Lord shall he behold: wherefore then were ye not afraid to speak against my servant Moses? And the anger of the Lord was kindled against them; and he departed."

God shows His anger when He departs from Aaron and Miriam in the next few verses, and we see Miriam stricken with leprosy as a result of the sins they committed in Numbers 12:10-11 KJV:

"And the cloud departed from off the tabernacle; and, behold, Miriam became leprous, white as snow: and Aaron looked upon Miriam, and, behold, she was leprous. And Aaron said unto Moses, Alas, my lord, I beseech thee, lay not the sin upon us, wherein we have done foolishly, and wherein we have sinned."

There's a question often asked with this set of verses: why was Miriam punished and Aaron not punished when Aaron acknowledges that he sinned as well? The statement to look at in understanding why Miriam received leprosy and not Aaron is found in the outcome of God's anger towards both in verses 9-10; the outcome of His anger shows what God intended to do. In God's anger towards Miriam and Aaron, He intended to render punishment and not death. God could have required their lives for their sins, but the outcome shows what God wanted to render in this situation, which was punishment. Additionally, because His intention was to give punishment, we further see God following the law system that He implemented for Israel being applied to Miriam's situation in Numbers 12:13-14 KJV:

"And Moses cried unto the Lord, saying, Heal her now, O God, I beseech thee. And the Lord said unto Moses, If her father had but spit in her face, should she not be ashamed seven days? Let her be shut out from the camp seven days, and after that let her be received in again."

We know that Miriam being shut out from the camp for seven days was in accordance with the law of Moses because this was the requirement God gave Israel for those with leprosy as recorded in Leviticus 13, which we will shortly see. This shows that God's intention with the punishment He gave was to follow the law system He gave Israel. Since this was God's intention, what we know about the law system is that the males were tasked with the leading role in executing the laws for Israel, primarily the males of the Levite tribe. With specific attention being given to Miriam, we see a scriptural example in Deuteronomy 24:8-9 KJV:

"Take heed in the plague of leprosy, that thou observe diligently, and do according to all that the priests the Levites shall teach you: as I commanded them, so ye shall observe to do. Remember what the Lord thy God did unto Miriam by the way, after that ye were come forth out of Egypt."

As we read this verse carefully in Deuteronomy 24:8-9, what is emphasized is the fact that the law of Moses was to be followed, and in this particular case, it dealt with the laws regarding leprosy. Miriam is given as the example to remember upon mentioning the commandments given to the priests pertaining to leprosy. This alerts us to the fact that, because it was God's intention to render punishment in His anger toward Miriam, and the punishment of leprosy was given to her, God, through this example, enforced that the law He put in place is to be obeyed. By Miriam taking the lead between her and Aaron in challenging Moses' leadership, she was trying to take a public role of influence among all of Israel, male and female simultaneously, that was outside of God's approval. Thus, by God saying Miriam is to be shut out from the camp for seven days due to her leprosy, it shows that she was to submit to her brother Aaron and his sons, who were the priests, in following God's implemented law for Israel. This also shows that her punishment was not only because she challenged God's order among her siblings Moses and Aaron, but also because she broke the authority/subjection law stated in 1 Corinthians 14:34 *"as also saith the law"* further explained in 1 Timothy 2:8-15, of which *"a woman is not allowed to teach or exercise authority over a man,"* which goes back to Adam and Eve. This is supported by Miriam's required submission to her brother Aaron as priest according to the Mosaic law.

Further evidence is seen in the book of Leviticus that the Law of Moses was to be followed to atone for the sins of Miriam and Aaron. First, with Miriam, the laws to follow regarding leprosy are found in Leviticus Chapters 13 and 14. We have the required standard in Leviticus 13:1-4 KJV:

"And the Lord spake unto Moses and Aaron, saying, When a man shall have in the skin of his flesh a rising, a scab, or bright spot, and it be in the skin of his flesh like the plague of leprosy; then he shall be brought unto Aaron the priest, or unto one of his sons the priests; and the priest shall look on the plague in the skin of the flesh: and when the hair in the plague is turned white, and the plague in sight be deeper than the skin of his flesh, it is a plague of leprosy: and the priest shall look on him and pronounce him unclean. If the bright spot be white in the skin of his flesh, and in sight be not deeper than the skin, and the hair thereof be not turned white; then the priest shall shut up him that hath the plague seven days."

With Leviticus chapter 13 covering the laws for leprosy, we see in chapter 14 the laws for cleansing the leper and making atonement for such. Emphasis is seen in Leviticus 14:10-20 KJV:

"And on the eighth day he shall take two he lambs without blemish, and one ewe lamb of the first year without blemish, and three tenth deals of fine flour for a meat offering, mingled with oil, and one log of oil. And the priest that maketh him clean shall present the man that is to be made clean, and those things, before the Lord, at the door of the tabernacle of the congregation And the priest shall take one he lamb, and offer him for a trespass offering, and the log of oil, and wave them for a wave offering before the Lord and he shall slay the lamb in the place where he shall kill the sin offering and the burnt offering, in the holy place: for as the sin offering is the priest's, so is the trespass offering: it is most holy and the priest shall take some of the blood of the trespass offering, and the priest shall put it upon the tip of the right ear of him that is to be cleansed, and upon the thumb of his right hand, and upon the great toe of his right foot And the priest shall take some of the log of oil, and pour it into the palm of his own left hand and the priest shall dip his right finger in the oil that is in his left hand, and shall sprinkle of the oil with his finger seven times before the Lord. And of the rest of the oil that is in his hand shall the priest put upon the tip of the right ear of him that is to be cleansed, and upon the thumb of his right hand, and upon the great toe of his right foot, upon the blood of the trespass offering. And the remnant of the oil that is in the priest's hand he shall pour upon the head of him that is to be cleansed: and the priest shall make an atonement for him before the Lord. And the priest shall offer the sin offering, and make an atonement for him that is to be cleansed from his uncleanness; and afterward he shall kill the burnt offering and the priest shall offer the burnt offering and the meat offering upon the altar: and the priest shall make an atonement for him, and he shall be clean."

As it pertains to the leprosy that God gave Miriam, for Miriam to receive atonement for her sins, the requirements of the law had to be fulfilled. The priest had to give a sin offering, burnt offering, and meat offering for an individual to be declared clean. Hence the reason in Deuteronomy 24:9, God tells Israel to listen to the commands He gave the priest on leprosy and to remember what He did to Miriam. By God implementing the law in Miriam's sin in Numbers 12, we see not only her required submission to the role of Moses, but we also see her required submission to the role of Aaron, who was high priest.

Additionally, we know Miriam and Aaron's sin in Numbers 12 was publicly known based on two statements; we again reference Deuteronomy 24:9, where the entire nation of Israel was to remember what the Lord thy God did unto Miriam. This references the leprosy as well as the reason God punished her with leprosy. Also, at the time Miriam was punished with leprosy, the entire Israeli nation did not journey until she was brought back in, as stated in Numbers 12:15-16 KJV:

"And Miriam was shut out from the camp seven days: and the people journeyed not till Miriam was brought in again. And afterward the people removed from Hazeroth, and pitched in the wilderness of Paran."

It was publicly known that she was stricken with leprosy by God; thus, an acknowledgment of the sin she committed was also publicly known by all of Israel. As it pertains to Aaron's sin in Numbers 12, because God implemented the law in Miriam's case, the same had to be done in Aaron's case. Aaron confessed to Moses that he sinned, as did Miriam, in Numbers 12:11 KJV:

"And Aaron said unto Moses, Alas, my lord, I beseech thee, lay not the sin upon us, wherein we have done foolishly, and wherein we have

sinned."

With this acknowledgment of sin by Aaron, in conjunction with God's implementation of the law for the atonement of Miriam's sin, it lets us know that Aaron also needed to have atonement for the sin that he committed according to the law of Moses. God gave instructions for how the high priest was to make atonement for his own sins before he could make atonement for the sins of any in Israel, and we see this law found in Leviticus 16:6-11 KJV:

"And Aaron shall offer his bullock of the sin offering, which is for himself, and make an atonement for himself, and for his house. And he shall take the two goats, and present them before the Lord at the door of the tabernacle of the congregation. And Aaron shall cast lots upon the two goats; one lot for the Lord, and the other lot for the scapegoat. And Aaron shall bring the goat upon which the Lord's lot fell, and offer him for a sin offering. But the goat, on which the lot fell to be the scapegoat, shall be presented alive before the Lord, to make an atonement with him, and to let him go for a scapegoat into the wilderness. And Aaron shall bring the bullock of the sin offering, which is for himself, and shall make an atonement for himself, and for his house, and shall kill the bullock of the sin offering which is for himself."

After the priest made atonement for his sins, atonement for the sins of Israel could be made, as seen in Leviticus 16:15-16 KJV:

"Then shall he kill the goat of the sin offering, that is for the people, and bring his blood within the vail, and do with that blood as he did with the blood of the bullock, and sprinkle it upon the mercy seat, and before the mercy seat and he shall make an atonement for the holy place, because of the uncleanness of the children of Israel, and because of their transgressions in all their sins: and so shall he do for the tabernacle of the congregation, that remaineth among them

in the midst of their uncleanness. And there shall be no man in the tabernacle of the congregation when he goeth in to make an atonement in the holy place, until he come out, and have made an atonement for himself, and for his household, and for all the congregation of Israel."

In Numbers 12:11, Aaron acknowledged he sinned; just because he didn't receive punishment when Miriam received leprosy did not resolve the sin of Aaron. Therefore, atonement had to be made to resolve his sin, and the only way for Aaron to have atonement for his sins was through the standard given to Israel, which is the law of Moses, specifically based on the verses we just mentioned.

Because Aaron had to follow the law in his sin with Miriam, and God implemented the law after Miriam was punished with leprosy, God, by Biblical example, enforces that the law He gives (specifically the authority/subjection law at the core of our study; enforced in the Old Testament and transcending into the Gospel of Christ in the New Testament) is to be followed at all times. As we've laid out with the example of Miriam, the authority/subjection law Paul discusses in 1 Corinthians 14:34 *"as also saith the law"* and 1 Timothy 2:8-15 was effective under the law of Moses and is still in effect within the Gospel of Christ. As it was initiated in the beginning: *"But I suffer not a woman to teach, nor to usurp authority over the man, but to be in silence. For Adam was first formed, then Eve. And Adam was not deceived, but the woman being deceived was in the transgression."*

Deborah

During a time in Israel's history when the nation did evil in the sight of the Lord and forgot the Lord God, serving Baalim and the groves (Judges 3:7), and would repeat evil in the sight of the Lord (Judges 4:1), Deborah was a prophetess and Judge. As we examine Deborah's time as Judge in Israel, there are two points that are imperative to our understanding of God's utilization of Deborah. The first is that the Law of Moses is God's covenant with Israel. In studying Exodus 24:4-8 KJV, we know this to be scripturally evident. As it states:

"And Moses wrote all the words of the Lord, and rose up early in the morning, and builded an altar under the hill, and twelve pillars, according to the twelve tribes of Israel. And he sent young men of the children of Israel, which offered burnt offerings, and sacrificed peace offerings of oxen unto the Lord. And Moses took half of the blood, and put it in basons; and half of the blood he sprinkled on the altar. And he took the book of the covenant, and read in the audience of the people: and they said, All that the Lord hath said will we do, and be obedient. And Moses took the blood, and sprinkled it on the people, and said, Behold the blood of the covenant, which the Lord hath made with you concerning all these words."

The second point is the fact that even during the time of Deborah, God's covenant was still in effect and never broken. For example, when we look into the book of Judges in chapter 2, verses 1 through 4, the Angel of the Lord spoke to Israel, confirming that He brought them out of Egypt into the land which He swore to their fathers and made the statement, "I will never break my covenant with you." However, because of Israel's disobedience to God's covenant, the nations that God was going to remove from the land that He gave to Israel became as thorns in their sides, and those gods a snare to Israel. Judges 2:1-4 KJV:

"And an angel of the Lord came up from Gilgal to Bochim, and said, I made you to go up out of Egypt, and have brought you unto the land which I sware unto your fathers; and I said, I will never break my covenant with you. And ye shall make no league with the inhabitants of this land; ye shall throw down their altars: but ye have not obeyed my voice: why have ye done this? Wherefore I also said, I will not drive them out from before you; but they shall be as thorns in your sides, and their gods shall be a snare unto you. And it came to pass, when the angel of the Lord spake these words unto all the children of Israel, that the people lifted up their voice, and wept."

This punishment coming from God was a statement made in God's covenant with Israel, seen in Numbers 33:55 KJV:

"But if ye will not drive out the inhabitants of the land from before you; then it shall come to pass, that those which ye let remain of them shall be pricks in your eyes, and thorns in your sides, and shall vex you in the land wherein ye dwell."

Even in Israel's punishment during the period of Judges, God was faithful to the covenant (the Law of Moses) He gave to Israel.

With this understanding of the Law of Moses being in full effect, meaning God never broke His word with Israel throughout the entirety of Israel's history, including the period of Judges, it is to be acknowledged that the Law made clear through God's instruction and example that the males solely held the role of public authority in teaching and speaking the word of God. Therefore, the question that is asked is how God is justified in using Deborah as Judge in Israel at one of Israel's lowest points without breaking His Law that He gave to

Israel? As apparently there were no righteous men available for use.

There are three points of emphasis that we bring your attention to in acknowledging God's utilization and instrumentation of Deborah, as the scriptures factually demonstrate how God always remained in accordance with His covenant with Israel through the Law of Moses. These three points are: the limits in Deborah's role as Prophetess and Judge, the functioning system known as the Law being part of the foundation of the Lord's church, and the omission of Deborah in Hebrews 11:32 & 1 Samuel 12:11. Let us begin by examining our first point.

Deborah - A Judge and Prophetess

It is evident in the reading of Judges 4:2-4 KJV that Deborah was a prophetess and Judge at the specific time of Israel's captivity into the hand of Jabin king of Canaan, whose army commander was Sisera. For twenty years, Jabin oppressed the sons of Israel, and it was during this time that Deborah sat under the palm tree of Deborah between Ramah and Bethel, and the sons of Israel came up to her for judgment. As it reads in Judges 4:2-5 KJV:

"And the Lord sold them into the hand of Jabin king of Canaan, that reigned in Hazor; the captain of whose host was Sisera, which dwelt in Harosheth of the Gentiles. And the children of Israel cried unto the Lord: for he had nine hundred chariots of iron; and twenty years he mightily oppressed the children of Israel. And Deborah, a prophetess, the wife of Lapidoth, she judged Israel at that time. And she dwelt

under the palm tree of Deborah between Ramah and Bethel in mount Ephraim: and the children of Israel came up to her for judgment."

It is at this set of scriptures that many use the case of Deborah for validation of women having public authority to teach men the gospel of Christ. However, as we've stated previously with Deborah and the period of Judges, God's covenant was still in effect, and God never broke His covenant. Therefore, Deborah was required to judge according to God's covenant with Israel (The Law of Moses). With God utilizing Deborah in having the sons of Israel come to her for judgment (Judges 4:5), Deborah was required to follow the instructions God gave to Israel for proper judgment, and this required a case-by-case hearing to give proper instruction in the judgment made. Thus, the judgment and instruction given by Deborah in accordance with the Law of Moses was conducted in a person-to-person setting, righteously hearing each case, and not public teaching to Israel as a whole. We initially see the example of giving proper and righteous judgment found in Moses. When Israel departed Egypt, there was a point when Moses spoke with his father-in-law Jethro, who noticed that the people stood by Moses from morning to evening. When Jethro asked Moses what is this thing you are doing, Moses replied that the people come to him to inquire of God; when they had a matter, Moses judged between one and another and made them know the statutes and laws of God, as seen in Exodus 18:13-16 KJV:

"And it came to pass on the morrow, that Moses sat to judge the people: and the people stood by Moses from the morning unto the evening. And when Moses' father in law saw all that he did to the people, he said, What is this thing that thou doest to the people? why sittest thou thyself alone, and all the people stand by thee from morning unto even? And Moses said unto his father in law, Because the people come unto me to enquire of God: when they have a matter, they come unto me;

and I judge between one and another, and I do make them know the statutes of God, and his laws."

Jethro, upon hearing this case-by-case judging on a matter between one and another done by Moses, offered advice to Moses so that he wouldn't wear away (Exodus 18:18). Jethro advised Moses to choose able, righteous men who feared God and teach them the ordinances and laws of God to judge the people at all seasons, and God would be with Moses in this implementation, of which Moses did all that Jethro advised. The hard cases were brought to Moses, who, being the prophet that God chose to lead all Israel, would give God's instruction in such hard cases (Exodus 18:19-26).

Additionally, the Law of Moses continues to show judgment was to be made righteously and without respect of persons, based on hearing each case, further confirming that judges in their role gave God's instruction in a person-to-person setting and not to the nation as a whole. This is seen in the following verses, Leviticus 19:15 KJV:

"Ye shall do no unrighteousness in judgment: thou shalt not respect the person of the poor, nor honor the person of the mighty: but in righteousness shalt thou judge thy neighbour."

Deuteronomy 1:16-17 KJV:
"And I charged your judges at that time, saying, Hear the causes between your brethren, and judge righteously between every man and his brother, and the stranger that is with him. Ye shall not respect persons in judgment; but ye shall hear the small as well as the great; ye shall not be afraid of the face of man; for the judgment is God's: and the cause that is too hard for you, bring it unto me, and I will hear it."

Deuteronomy 16:18-19 KJV:

"Judges and officers shalt thou make thee in all thy gates, which the Lord thy God giveth thee, throughout thy tribes: and they shall judge the people with just judgment. Thou shalt not wrest judgment; thou shalt not respect persons, neither take a gift: for a gift doth blind the eyes of the wise, and pervert the words of the righteous."

Deuteronomy 17:8-9 KJV:

"If there arise a matter too hard for thee in judgment, between blood and blood, between plea and plea, and between stroke and stroke, being matters of controversy within thy gates: then shalt thou arise, and get thee up into the place which the Lord thy God shall choose. And thou shalt come unto the priests the Levites, and unto the judge that shall be in those days, and enquire; and they shall shew thee the sentence of judgment."

And Deuteronomy 25:1-2 KJV:

"If there be a controversy between men, and they come unto judgment, that the judges may judge them; then they shall justify the righteous, and condemn the wicked. And it shall be, if the wicked man be worthy to be beaten, that the judge shall cause him to lie down, and to be beaten before his face, according to his fault, by a certain number."

As Deborah is judge during the time of Israel's bondage to Jabin king of Canaan, this is the required standard that she was to follow in judging according to the Law (God's covenant); a case-by-case judging which required righteously hearing the matter without respect of persons in each case, which is a person-to-person setting. Furthermore, the mention of Deborah as a prophetess informs us that she spoke with God's authority to provide instruction and judgment for such hard cases that were presented, similar to the hard cases that were presented to Moses, who was a prophet of God speaking with His authority in providing God's instruction to resolve those hard cases. God continues to show us how He utilized Deborah in her role as a prophetess, as she summoned Barak to convey God's commandment to him in Judges 4:6 KJV:

"And she sent and called Barak the son of Abinoam out of Kedeshnaphtali, and said unto him, Hath not the Lord God of Israel commanded, saying, Go and draw toward mount Tabor, and take with thee ten thousand men of the children of Naphtali and of the children of Zebulun?"

In examining this verse, Deborah is continuing to be utilized by God in a person-to-person setting in her role as prophetess when she instructs Barak on the commandment given to him by God. This is evident by the fact that she sent for Barak to come to her in order to convey this commandment to him face to face. What is evident in studying this information pertaining to Deborah in her roles as Judge and Prophetess is that her functioning in these roles had a specific boundary of approval as she is utilized by God, thus meaning God has given approval to Deborah to instruct men in a person-to-person setting as opposed to the public platform that God gave to the prophets and men according to the Law. This is further evident as we contrast Deborah's usage in Judges 4 with the public speaking of the prophet to all Israel in Judges 6:7-10 KJV:

"And it came to pass, when the children of Israel cried unto the Lord because of the Midianites, that the Lord sent a prophet unto the children of Israel, which said unto them, Thus saith the Lord God of Israel, I brought you up from Egypt, and brought you forth out of the house of bondage; and I delivered you out of the hand of the Egyptians, and out of the hand of all that oppressed you, and drave them out from before you, and gave you their land; and I said unto you, I am the Lord your God; fear not the gods of the Amorites, in whose land ye dwell:

but ye have not obeyed my voice."

This further demonstrates God's intention in the statement made by Paul in 1 Corinthians 14:34 "as also saith the law" and 1 Timothy 2:11-15, covering every facet of publicly teaching the word of God; evident in the specific boundary of His usage of Deborah versus His public usage of the prophets.

Huldah and Priscillia

This specific boundary is not only seen with Deborah, but also with the other two women in scripture that are seen instructing the word of God to men, the prophetess Huldah and Aquila's wife Priscilla. In both cases, as with Deborah, they are not publicly proclaiming the word of God to the masses of male and female simultaneously. Huldah is seen in 2 Kings 22:12-17 KJV:

"And the king commanded Hilkiah the priest, and Ahikam the son of Shaphan, and Achbor the son of Michaiah, and Shaphan the scribe, and Asahiah a servant of the king's, saying go ye, enquire of the Lord for me, and for the people, and for all Judah, concerning the words of this book that is found: for great is the wrath of the Lord that is kindled against us, because our fathers have not hearkened unto the words of this book, to do according unto all that which is written concerning us. So Hilkiah the priest, and Ahikam, and Achbor, and Shaphan, and Asahiah, went unto Huldah the prophetess, the wife of Shallum the son of Tikvah, the son of Harhas, keeper of the wardrobe; (now she dwelt in Jerusalem in the college;) and they communed with her. And she said unto them, Thus saith the Lord God of Israel, Tell the man that

sent you to me, thus saith the Lord, Behold, I will bring evil upon this place, and upon the inhabitants thereof, even all the words of the book which the king of Judah hath read because they have forsaken me, and have burned incense unto other gods, that they might provoke me to anger with all the works of their hands; therefore my wrath shall be kindled against this place, and shall not be quenched."

Comparing Huldah and Deborah in their roles as prophetesses, we see the same standard applied to how they functioned in their role, which is in the absence of the public platform while speaking God's commandments to men, thus showing how they functioned is the approved standard by God. With Huldah, she did not publicly proclaim what thus saith the Lord for the people, nor all of Judah; but men came to her residence in the college in Jerusalem, and she told them the word of God, those men were to proclaim to the King, for the people, and all of Judah the Lord's commandments. Barak, in like manner, came to Deborah, and then the commandment of the Lord was spoken to him. Deborah and Huldah were able to teach the men they were speaking to, the commandments of God in a setting that did not include the public platform. This is the scriptural standard that we see being applied with Deborah and Huldah as they functioned in their approved roles as prophetesses of God. Therefore, to go beyond this God-approved standard of how the women of scripture functioned in teaching is to act beyond what is seen in scripture; also known as acting beyond the scriptural authority from God.

Additionally, we also see this same standard applied with Priscilla, the wife of Aquila in the New Testament in Acts 18:24-26 KJV:

"And a certain Jew named Apollos, born at Alexandria, an eloquent man, and mighty in the scriptures, came to Ephesus. This man was instructed in the way of the Lord; and being fervent in the spirit, he

spake and taught diligently the things of the Lord, knowing only the baptism of John. And he began to speak boldly in the synagogue: whom when Aquila and Priscilla had heard, they took him unto them, and expounded unto him the way of God more perfectly."

Priscilla was able to help Aquila teach Apollos by giving a detailed explanation of the gospel more perfectly, which defines the Greek word ektithēmi (expounded) in Acts 18:26. Yet notice that this teaching was not done publicly, and it falls in line with the non-public teaching of God's word to men that Deborah and Huldah committed themselves to; in a person-to-person setting. It's important to acknowledge that Aquila and Priscilla were Jews that obeyed the gospel of Christ. We know this much according to Acts 18:2 KJV:

"And found a certain Jew named Aquila, born in Pontus, lately come from Italy, with his wife Priscilla; (because that Claudius had commanded all Jews to depart from Rome:) and came unto them."

With that said, by the simple mention of Aquila and Priscilla being Jews, there is the implication of them having knowledge of how God used women in history to speak His word to men with His approval, based on God's word within the Old Testament, which these two Jewish individuals followed prior to obeying the Gospel of Christ. The fact that Priscilla followed the exact example of how Deborah spoke in a person-to-person setting with Barak and how Huldah also spoke in a person-to-person setting with Hilkiah, Ahikam, Achbor, Shaphan, and Asahiah within her residence gives the implication that Aquila and Priscilla were aware of how God enforced His law under the Old Testament and followed the pattern of these women recorded in God's word. Submitting herself to the law the apostle Paul speaks of in 1 Corinthians 14:34 KJV:

"as also saith the law"

And 1 Timothy 2:12-13 KJV:

"But I suffer not a woman to teach, nor to usurp authority over the man, but to be in silence. For Adam was first formed, then Eve."

Additionally, it has been said that the reason Aquila and Priscilla took Apollos to themselves and taught him more perfectly is that Apollos sinned in his teaching, and they brought the sinful offense to him, using the standard Jesus taught in Matthew 18:15-18 KJV:

"Moreover if thy brother shall trespass against thee, go and tell him his fault between thee and him alone: if he shall hear thee, thou hast gained thy brother. But if he will not hear thee, then take with thee one or two more, that in the mouth of two or three witnesses every word may be established. And if he shall neglect to hear them, tell it unto the church: but if he neglect to hear the church, let him be unto thee as an heathen man and a publican. Verily I say unto you, Whatsoever ye shall bind on earth shall be bound in heaven: and whatsoever ye shall loose on earth shall be loosed in heaven."

However, Matthew 18:15-18 does not apply here with what Aquila and Priscilla did with Apollos. The teaching that Apollos did in the synagogue in Acts 18 was done publicly; what Matthew 18:15-18 teaches is the standard to be applied when there is a personal offense committed by one brother to another, meaning the offense is not publicly known. The first step is to tell the fault between the two alone; then a gradual progression of making brethren aware is to be taken if the brother will not hear; that is, taking one or two more witnesses that every word may be established; if the brother still neglects to hear, then it is made public to the church. Every word that Apollos spoke in the synagogue was publicly established to all in the synagogue who heard him speak. Aquila and Priscilla are following a standard evident in scripture when a woman is involved in teaching, and that standard is seen in the example of the prophetesses Deborah and Huldah within the Old Testament.

The Functioning Law System in the Foundation of the Lord's church

God's covenant, the Law of Moses, was a public functioning legal system. While the Law included rules and regulations conducive to maintaining order, settling disputes, and facilitating peace, it was also God's word in establishing His standard. The quality of the individuals He chose to enforce His standard, that being His legal system, confirms that the quality of those individuals met His standard. Scripture confirms that this public functioning legal system was established by God in view of Christ and His church. Thus, the quality of the individuals chosen by God to enforce His standard within this public functioning legal system, the Law of Moses, must meet the quality of standard held within the public functioning of the Lord's church.

As we continue to examine Deborah and God's usage of her, a critical yet often overlooked fact about the Law of Moses, of which Deborah lived faithfully under, is that the Mosaic Law is part of the foundation of the Lord's church. There are three sets of scriptures that I bring to your attention that make this fact evident. Romans 3:21 KJV:

"But now the righteousness of God without the law is manifested, being witnessed by the law and the prophets"

Ephesians 2:19-20 KJV:
"Now therefore ye are no more strangers and foreigners, but

fellowcitizens with the saints, and of the household of God and are built upon the foundation of the apostles and prophets, Jesus Christ himself being the chief corner stone."

And Hebrews 6:1-2 KJV:

"Therefore leaving the principles of the doctrine of Christ, let us go on unto perfection; not laying again the foundation of repentance from dead works, and of faith toward God of the doctrine of baptisms, and of laying on of hands, and of resurrection of the dead, and of eternal judgment."

The Law of Moses is the beginning teachings of the doctrine (teaching) of Christ, the prophets prophesied (taught) to Israel about the coming of Christ, and the church is built on the foundation (teaching) of the apostles and prophets. The critical fact in these verses and statements is that the law, prophets, and apostles are all publicly teaching the church about Christ. This means the system known as the Law of Moses was a public function in its laws, ordinances, and observances, all of which taught of a time of fulfillment to be had in Christ, as what was done under the Mosaic Law was "a shadow of good things to come not the very image." (Hebrews 10:1). Therefore, those who functioned publicly within that system of the Law of Moses are publicly teaching the church through the scriptures that the Law testified of the righteousness of God without the Law (Rom. 3:21), as it is the beginning teachings of Christ. Yet, 1 Corinthians 14:34 and 1 Timothy 2:11-15 forbids the woman from authoritatively teaching the men. Thus, to say Deborah publicly taught or led Israel within the Law of Moses is to say that she was given a public role in Israel by God, thereby having public authority in teaching the Lord's church; as the Law is the beginning teachings of Christ and the prophets are part of the foundation of the Lord's church.

SCRIPTURALLY CAN WOMEN USE PUBLIC PLATFORMS TO TEACH MEN THE GOSPEL OF CHRIST?

The Omission of Deborah in 1 Samuel 12:11 & Hebrews 11:32

As we continue to keep in mind that God never broke His covenant with Israel, there are two sets of verses that show a difference with Deborah as judge compared to the other Judges mentioned within these sets of scripture. The first set of scripture is 1 Samuel 12:11 KJV:

"And the Lord sent Jerubbaal, and Bedan, and Jephthah, and Samuel, and delivered you out of the hand of your enemies on every side, and ye dwelled safe."

And the second set of scripture is Hebrews 11:32 KJV:

"And what shall I more say? for the time would fail me to tell of Gedeon, and of Barak, and of Samson, and of Jephthae; of David also, and Samuel, and of the prophets."

Why does the inspired word of God omit Deborah yet place Barak in these verses when the Judges mentioned include Deborah's time period?

One may be led to believe that Barak being mentioned and not Deborah in these verses is due to a simple case of acknowledging military leaders who led the charge of Israel in conquering the other nations. However, this is not the case due to the scriptural fact that Samuel was not a military leader. The mentioning of Samuel and Barak, along with the rest of the men in both of these verses, scripturally shows that this is a case of having public authority. The mention of these individuals, who were tasked with different functions yet leading Israel against their enemies, confirms they had a specific quality that met God's standard in having His authority to lead Israel in conquering these nations.

There are two scriptural facts of understanding that we will discuss pertaining to the Law, which these sets of scripture are leading us to; that being the specific quality each individual in these verses had is the fact that they were men, thus meeting God's standard for public authority to lead Israel. First is the executing of burnt offerings and the second is divine order.

Executing of Burnt Offerings

As we look at Samuel being mentioned in these verses, it is scripturally acknowledged that Samuel judged Israel, as seen in 1 Samuel 7:15 KJV:
"And Samuel judged Israel all the days of his life."

Yet, unlike Barak, Gideon, and Jephthah, Samuel did not physically lead the charge in the fight against the enemies of Israel. However, Samuel did lead Israel in the fight against the Philistines by executing a requirement of the Law, that being the burnt offering for the sins of Israel; as seen in 1 Samuel 7:8-11 KJV:
"And the children of Israel said to Samuel, Cease not to cry unto the Lord our God for us, that he will save us out of the hand of the Philistines. And Samuel took a sucking lamb, and offered it for a burnt offering wholly unto the Lord: and Samuel cried unto the Lord for Israel; and the Lord heard him. And as Samuel was offering up the burnt offering, the Philistines drew near to battle against Israel: but the Lord thundered with a great thunder on that day upon the Philistines, and discomfited them; and they were smitten before Israel. And the men of Israel went out of Mizpeh, and pursued the Philistines, and smote them, until they came under Bethcar."

The execution of the burnt offering by Samuel is what God accepted for the sins of Israel, and God moved in response to this by acting on Samuel's prayer for Israel, giving Israel victory over the Philistines. This is significant for two reasons: the first being that the term burnt offering is the Hebrew term 'ôlâh 'ôlâh and is defined as "going up in smoke" and "ascending." Thus, the burnt offering was a public proclamation of sacrifice in the shedding of blood for the atonement of sins, which was done in seeking acceptance by God and in worship. The most crucial point in this fact is that the burnt offering, with its public proclamation, was a foreshadowing of the sacrifice of Christ (Hebrews 10:1-10); thus, it was a public teaching of the forthcoming Messiah, who would be the ultimate atonement for the sins of the world. The Law of Moses required the men to execute the burnt offerings, which was a public teaching of Christ.

The second reason for the significance of the burnt offering by Samuel is that, unlike Deborah, Gideon shared in the act of executing a burnt offering as Samuel did, and Jephthah had the ability to exercise a burnt offering to the Lord as Samuel did. The following two verses confirm this fact: Judges 6:25-27 KJV:

"And it came to pass the same night, that the Lord said unto him, Take thy father's young bullock, even the second bullock of seven years old, and throw down the altar of Baal that thy father hath, and cut down the grove that is by it: and build an altar unto the Lord thy God upon the top of this rock, in the ordered place, and take the second bullock, and offer a burnt sacrifice with the wood of the grove which thou shalt cut down. Then Gideon took ten men of his servants, and did as the Lord had said unto him: and so it was, because he feared his father's household, and the men of the city, that he could not do it by day, that he did it by night."

And Judges 11:30-31 KJV:

"And Jephthah vowed a vow unto the Lord, and said, If thou shalt without fail deliver the children of Ammon into mine hands, then it shall be, that whatsoever cometh forth of the doors of my house to meet me, when I return in peace from the children of Ammon, shall surely be the Lord's, and I will offer it up for a burnt offering."

During the time of Gideon, Israel was being oppressed by the Midianites. For the Lord to work through Gideon in saving Israel from the Midianites, atonement for sins through the requirement of the Law had to be executed; thus, a burnt offering was commanded by the Lord.

During the time of Jephthah, the Ammonites waged war against Israel, accusing Israel of taking their land. Jephthah tried reasoning with the king of Ammon by sending messengers to explain that Israel hadn't taken their land and displayed three points of knowledge: knowledge of Israel's history (Judges 11:12-25), knowledge of the Lord the Judge (Judges 11:27), and knowledge of the Law of Moses (Judges 11:30-31).

Jephthah was very aware of the requirements of the Law of Moses as he made a vow in giving one of two sacrifices of what greets him upon his return according to the Law (i.e., dedication to the Lord or burnt offering) in verses 31-32; in his vow, he makes the statement that *"whatsoever cometh forth of the doors of my house to meet me, when I return in peace from the children of Ammon, shall surely be the Lord's, and I will offer it up for a burnt offering."* The vow law is seen in Leviticus 27:28. Jephthah's knowledge of vowing a burnt offering shows he was aware that he met the quality of standard established by God to present this option of sacrifice. Ultimately, his only child, being his firstborn, his daughter met him, and she was dedicated to God's service that was lifelong at the tabernacle. Evident by the facts of the Law of Moses that only sacrificial animals could be placed on the altar, everything else was placed into God's service or redeemed. Furthermore, it is stated in Judges 11:39 that *"he did with her according to his vow and she knew no man"* (i.e., sexual relations); it said nothing of her dying after the vow (See Anna the prophetess, for women working at the tabernacle).

What is seen of Samuel, Gideon, and Jephthah is something that Deborah was not capable of doing according to the Law of Moses. Deborah did not have the ability to execute burnt offerings to atone for the sins of Israel according to the Law; thus, she could not publicly lead Israel, which is why we see the omission of Deborah in 1 Samuel 12:11 and Hebrews 11:32, with Barak listed instead.

Divine Order

As we scripturally see the facts of God's word presented to us, one may still ask why Barak is listed in 1 Samuel 12:11 and Hebrews 11:32? Even though it is seen that Samuel wasn't a military leader, yet he was a judge who executed burnt offerings as the other Judge Gideon did, and Jephthah had the ability to do so. Barak did not execute a burnt offering, nor was he a Judge. However, as Barak is listed with these judges, it is important to our understanding that what is said of one of these individuals in deliverance from Israel's enemies is also meant for every individual judge listed in these sets of scripture, as it also equals the Divine order of God's authority. There is a statement made to Jephthah from the elders of Gilead, that being *"be our head"*, as seen in Judges 11:8 KJV, as they sought him out to fight against the

Ammonites:

"And the elders of Gilead said unto Jephthah, therefore we turn again to thee now, that thou mayest go with us, and fight against the children of Ammon, and be our head over all the inhabitants of Gilead."

God gave equal deliverance to Israel by sending Gideon, Barak, Jephthah, and Samuel; therefore, what is said of one of these individuals (i.e., Jephthah) to be the head over all in deliverance equally applies to every individual listed, void of the limits of being known as a military leader, as Samuel was not one. For these men to be head over all is an acknowledgment that these individuals led Israel as the public authority representatives of God to the nations as they conquered their enemies. This is evident in the fact that this also meets God's divine order as stated in 1 Corinthians 11:3 KJV:

"But I would have you know, that the head of every man is Christ; and the head of the woman is the man; and the head of Christ is God."

As we examine this statement made by Paul in 1 Corinthians, we see an immutable fact: meaning a standard that is not capable of being changed; that is the range of God the Father's authority. God has complete power, authority, and rule and is head over all, as this is a part of the nature of God. This completeness of God can never be substituted (not even temporarily), replaced, nor removed. Therefore, His word always stands as the rule of authority for all, and that can never be changed. This is the premise of 1 Corinthians 11:3. With these facts in mind pertaining to the order seen in this verse, God implements the standard of authority seen based on the quality of the individuals listed under Him. The range of authority He gives encompasses complete authority operating from and established in God's rule and instruction; in every facet of life accordant with the quality of those individuals, they are listed as head over. Therefore, the authority given to the quality of the individuals in the order presented under God the Father can never be substituted (not even temporarily), replaced, nor removed; and this strictly comes from the immutable nature of God.

Meaning Christ has complete authority over every man and every woman; evident in the fact that if any human wants to obtain salvation, they must submit to Jesus Christ, as Acts 4:12 KJV says:
"Neither is their salvation in any other for there is none other name under Heaven given among men whereby we must be saved."

As Jesus is the only way to God the Father, as stated by Jesus in John 14:6 KJV:
"I am the way, the truth, and the life: no man cometh unto the Father but by Me."

This authority given to Jesus Christ has been implemented by God's choice, and that range of authority is for all under Christ in every facet of life, thereby making His authority public. In like manner, the man has complete authority accordant with the quality of individuals listed under him, this being the woman. This is evident in God's choice of implementing the man over the woman in every facet of life requiring public authority and leadership, seen throughout every age in history throughout the scriptures. For example, as seen in God's choice of Noah in the Patriarchal age to lead seven souls other than himself to save the human race; a man that found grace in the eyes of the Lord and was a preacher of righteousness; Genesis 6:8 KJV:
"But Noah found grace in the eyes of the Lord."

And 2 Peter 2:5 KJV:
"And spared not the old world, but saved Noah the eighth, a preacher

of righteousness bringing in the flood upon the world of the ungodly."

This is also seen in the Mosaic age. It is clear that God chose the man Moses to lead Israel out of Egypt; yet, the man's headship over the woman is also seen in the legal public life of Israel as God required men to be elders and officers over the people, Numbers 11:16 KJV:

"And the Lord said unto Moses, gather me seventy men of the elders of Israel, whom thou knowest to be elders of the people, and officers over them; and bring them unto the tabernacle of the congregation, that they may stand there with thee."

Additionally, this fact was known outside of Israel, with the priest of Midian known as a friend of God by his name Reuel (Exodus 2:16-18), whom we've previously stated is also Moses' father-in-law Jethro (Exodus 18:12). We bring you back to the statements of Jethro who gave Moses counsel to properly judge Israel in choosing men who feared God to judge the people; in doing this, God would be with him. Exodus 18:19-22 KJV:

"Hearken now unto my voice, I will give thee counsel, and God shall be with thee: Be thou for the people to God-ward, that thou mayest bring the causes unto God: And thou shalt teach them ordinances and laws, and shalt shew them the way wherein they must walk, and the work that they must do. Moreover thou shalt provide out of all the people able men, such as fear God, men of truth, hating covetousness; and place such over them, to be rulers of thousands, and rulers of hundreds, rulers of fifties, and rulers of tens: And let them judge the people at all seasons: and it shall be, that every great matter they shall bring unto thee, but every small matter they shall judge: so shall it be easier for thyself, and they shall bear the burden with thee."

And lastly, this is seen under the gospel of Christ; the Christian age, with statements made by the inspired apostle Paul confirming the Godly order, standard, and effective time of man's headship over the woman; 1 Corinthians 11:3 KJV:

"But I would have you know, that the head of every man is Christ; and the head of the woman is the man; and the head of Christ is God."

And 1 Timothy 2:11-15 KJV:

"Let the woman learn in silence with all subjection. But I suffer not a woman to teach, nor to usurp authority over the man, but to be in silence. For Adam was first formed, then Eve. And Adam was not deceived, but the woman being deceived was in the transgression. Notwithstanding she shall be saved in childbearing, if they continue in faith and charity and holiness with sobriety."

Which is *"as also saith the law"* (1 Corinthians 14:34). Therefore, as we look at the omission of Deborah and insertion of Barak in 1 Samuel 12:11 and Hebrews 11:32, it is because God's authority given to man over woman can never be substituted (not even temporarily), replaced, nor removed.

6

Women Who Labored in the Temple and the Gospel of Christ

Anna The Prophetess

Yet, some may look to Luke 2:36-38 KJV with Anna the Prophetess as a scriptural example of public teaching authority for women, as it says:

"And there was one Anna, a prophetess, the daughter of Phanuel, of the tribe of Aser: she was of a great age, and had lived with an husband seven years from her virginity; and she was a widow of about fourscore and four years, which departed not from the temple, but served God with fastings and prayers night and day. and she coming in that instant gave thanks likewise unto the Lord, and spake of him to all them that looked for redemption in Jerusalem."

Based on this set of scriptures, some individuals may come to one of two conclusions regarding her being a prophetess who didn't depart from the temple. First, one may suggest that here we have an example of a Prophetess teaching the word of God to both men and women, as she is in the temple in Jerusalem where God commanded worship from physical Israel. However, what is seen in verse 39 gives us insight into Anna the Prophetess in the Temple. Luke 2:39 KJV:

"And when they had performed all things according to the law of the Lord,"

Yes, this verse is talking about Joseph and Mary, who performed all things according to the law of the Lord before returning to Galilee, to Nazareth. However, an individual under the Law of Moses who had authority from God; in this case, it is Anna the Prophetess, must perform all things according to the law of the Lord. As we specifically place emphasis on the woman Anna, who was a prophetess in the temple, there was a specific location where women were to serve in the temple, according to how it was implemented under the Law of Moses, and we have scriptural examples given to us in the following two verses:

Exodus 38:8 KJV:
"And he made the laver of brass, and the foot of it of brass, of the looking glasses of the women assembling, which assembled at the door of the tabernacle of the congregation."

And 1 Samuel 2:22 KJV:
"Now Eli was very old, and heard all that his sons did unto all Israel; and how they lay with the women that assembled at the door of the tabernacle of the congregation."

Though the tabernacle of the congregation was temporary, it was the precursor to the temple, of which both were the dwelling places of God. Thus, meaning the Law of Moses was applied the same way in both locations, and what is seen with the women at the tabernacle of the congregation is the fact that the women had a specific location where they served, and with each scriptural example, they were not given authority to publicly teach men. Instead, we see God using Moses in Exodus 38:8, and Eli's sons are the authority in 1 Samuel 2:22. Therefore, following the pattern seen in these scriptural examples under the Law of Moses, which were not to be transgressed, we know Anna the Prophetess served in a specific location in the temple specifically for women and not to an audience mixed with male and female Jews.

Second, one may suggest that this confirms the restrictions seen in 1 Corinthians 14:34 and 1 Timothy 2:11-15 are confined to the order of worship; therefore, women can have public authority to teach men outside of worship. However, there was a time in physical Israel's history in the Old Testament when there was neither tabernacle of the congregation nor temple, as it was destroyed and had to be rebuilt due to Israel's sins, which brought about the punishment of captivity.

Yet, during this time when there was no temple, God's word was publicly spoken to Israel, and the enforcement by God in choosing men to publicly proclaim His word shows all who had the authority to lead Israel in helping them to preserve their faith. Thereby, confirming that the realm of use of the prophet to operate publicly by God's authority reached beyond the worship setting and into the arenas of society. As we give a scriptural example at the start of the rebuilding of the temple in Ezra 5:1-2 KJV:

"Then the prophets, Haggai the prophet, and Zechariah the son of Iddo, prophesied unto the Jews that were in Judah and Jerusalem in the name of the God of Israel, even unto them. Then rose up Zerubbabel the son of Shealtiel, and Jeshua the son of Jozadak, and began to build the

house of God which is at Jerusalem: and with them were the prophets of God helping them."

As we view the example of God's implementation of the Law in using His prophets, we reiterate the point that the law and the prophets form the beginning foundation of Christ, as we've discussed with Hebrews 6:1 and Ephesians 2:20. Therefore, we are to realize the principle enforced by God. Physical Israel under the Law of Moses is the figure of spiritual Israel, the Lord's church, under the gospel of Christ. With emphasis on the authority to teach and lead, God teaches man through the beginning foundation laid of physical Israel how spiritual Israel is to operate. God's implementation of the prophets and not the prophetesses on every public platform in the figure of physical Israel confirms that the principle enforced by God under the Old Law is exactly how the principle is to be enforced under the gospel of Christ, of which the principle is seen in the statement of 1 Corinthians 14:34 *"as also saith the law"* and 1 Timothy 2:11-15 **But I suffer not a woman to teach, nor to usurp authority over the man, but to be in silence. For Adam was first formed, then Eve. And Adam was not deceived, but the woman being deceived was in the transgression.** A principle that has stood from the beginning with Adam and Eve, which we will see in the chapter on Genesis.

Euodias and Syntyche

However, objections may occur based on what the apostle Paul said of two women named Euodias and Syntyche in Philippians 4:2-3 KJV:
"I beseech Euodias, and beseech Syntyche, that they be of the same

mind in the Lord. And I intreat thee also, true yokefellow, help those women which laboured with me in the gospel, with Clement also, and with other my fellowlabourers, whose names are in the book of life."

Paul here mentions the fact that Euodias and Syntyche labored with him; but not just Paul only. These two women also labored with Clement and with other fellow laborers of Paul. The thought being that Paul labored in preaching and teaching the gospel, and he presents a fact that Euodias and Syntyche labored with him; therefore, some may conclude that these women mentioned by Paul also labored in preaching and teaching the gospel. Thus, some conclude that women have the authority to teach men publicly since they labored with Paul. However, there are three facts of scripture that we must acknowledge pertaining to what is mentioned in these verses regarding Euodias and Syntyche in rightly dividing the word of truth.

First, as we look at the role that Euodias and Syntyche had in their labor with Paul, it is very important that the divine message of the gospel of Christ is correctly dissected with the arguments that are put forth in defense of the Lord's teachings. With that said, the command given by the apostle Paul in 1 Timothy 2:11-15 is a fact that goes against the thought that Euodias and Syntyche publicly taught men the gospel of Christ, as these women would have authority to teach over the men present with them, meaning Paul, Clement, and other of Paul's fellow laborers; which goes against the command given by the Lord through Paul for women to learn in silence with all subjection and not to teach nor to have authority over the man but to be in silence (1 Timothy 2:11-12).

Second, as we look at what Paul said of Euodias and Syntyche in Philippians 4:3 and compare it with what is said of Clement and other companions of Paul in this very same verse, there is a difference in the terms that are used here. Paul says Euodias and Syntyche labored (**sunathleō**) with him while Clement and the others were Paul's fellow laborers (**sunergos**). The significance of the difference in the usage of the terms is that the latter term sunergos is defined as a co-laborer. In other words, there is a shared action and participation that Paul had with Clement and the others mentioned in Philippians 4:3. The thirteen times the word sunergos is used in the New Testament scriptures, it is in reference to either individuals who shared an action with Paul in the gospel or a call for brethren to share an action in the gospel; that action being a co-laborer of the truth as seen in 3 John 1:8 KJV:

"We therefore ought to receive such, that we might be fellowhelpers to the truth."

Thus, the usage of the term sunergos describes one who shares the action of teaching the truth in Christ, just as Paul taught the truth in Christ. Additionally, as this term is applied to Priscilla and Aquila in Romans 16:3, the fact must be stated: the only scriptural example given to us of the teaching Priscilla did was with her husband Aquila and was in a person-to-person setting and not done publicly [Acts 18:25-26]. Therefore, not going beyond what is scripturally written, Priscilla meets the commands found in the New Testament in 1 Corinthians 14:34 and 1 Timothy 2:11-15. More is discussed on Priscilla in the chapter on Prophetesses and Priscilla. As it pertains to Euodias and Syntyche in Philippians 4:3, the usage of the term sunergos (fellow laborers), which is applied to individuals who share the labor of teaching the truth in Christ, was not applied by Paul to these women and the labor they committed themselves to. Therefore, scripturally speaking, Euodias and Syntyche did not publicly teach men.

Third, when we look at the term (**sunathleō**) which is applied by Paul to Euodias and Syntyche in describing the labor these women committed themselves to, it is defined as a striving together for. This word is used only one other time in the New Testament scriptures, which is in the very letter we are examining with Euodias and Syntyche; that being Philippians 1:27. As Paul is addressing all the saints in Christ Jesus at Philippi, with the bishops and deacons (Philippians 1:1), to be with one mind striving for the faith of the gospel. As it reads in Philippians 1:27 KJV:

"Only let your conversation be as it becometh the gospel of Christ: that whether I come and see you, or else be absent, I may hear of your affairs, that ye stand fast in one spirit, with one mind striving together for the faith of the gospel."

This alerts us to a fact that is often overlooked; that being there are other forms of labor in Christ other than preaching and teaching the gospel, which is inclusive of both male and female. As Paul tells the Philippians to be with one mind, all were to equally have the mind to put into action all the teachings of Christ Jesus in their daily lives, which manifests in the church having the common ground of working together for the faith of the gospel (all the principles that Christ teaches).

Given our first two factual points concerning these women, in addition to our third point being made here, as we look at Euodias and Syntyche, the labor these women committed themselves to is confirmed to be a labor in the gospel that was separate from the authority had in publicly teaching men the gospel of Christ. Yet, the labor these women committed themselves to was also a labor that Paul committed himself to in the gospel; as Paul confirms in Philippians 4:3 KJV:

"help those women which laboured with me in the gospel."

SCRIPTURALLY CAN WOMEN USE PUBLIC PLATFORMS TO TEACH MEN THE GOSPEL OF CHRIST?

There are two sets of verses I call your attention to which confirm the labor Euodias and Syntyche worked together with Paul in was a labor the church as a whole is to work together in.

Hebrews 6:10-11 KJV:

"For God is not unrighteous to forget your work and labour of love, which ye have shewed toward his name, in that ye have ministered to the saints, and do minister. And we desire that every one of you do shew the same diligence to the full assurance of hope unto the end."

And Romans 16:6 KJV:

"Greet Mary, who bestowed much labour on us."

In Hebrews 6:10-11, the writer of Hebrews says God will not forget the work and labor those Christians showed towards His name in ministering to the saints, and the writer encourages every one of those Christians he is writing to; to show the same eagerness of work and labor of love towards God's name in ministering to the saints. Additionally, in Romans 16:6, there was a sister in Christ named Mary who worked hard on behalf of Christians. Thus, we conclude that the labor that Euodias and Syntyche committed themselves to was a labor that all Christians are to work together in; this is also a labor that Paul committed himself to as a Christian (Romans 15:25); that being a labor of service.

Philip's Four Daughters Who Prophesied

There are some individuals who have made a defense of women publicly teaching men the gospel of Christ by one specific set of verses found in Acts 21:8-9 KJV:

"And the next day we that were of Paul's company departed, and came unto Caesarea: and we entered into the house of Philip the evangelist, which was one of the seven; and abode with him. And the same man had four daughters, virgins, which did prophesy."

With particular emphasis on verse nine, the statement acknowledging Philip's four virgin daughters who prophesied is viewed by some as giving women authority to publicly teach both men and women God's word. However, as we take a closer look at the context of Acts 20-21, along with what is said in the verses immediately following Acts 21:9, and compare it with the command found in the statement *"as also saith the law"* (1 Corinthians 14:34), which is established in the explanation given in 1 Timothy 2:11-15, a picture of scriptural facts is painted showing the limitations that were authorized by God in the authority He gave Philip's daughters to prophesy.

The first statement that is mentioned in Acts 21:8 is *"And the next day we."* This information shows that the individual who wrote this epistle was with Paul at the time that Paul entered the house of Philip. It is widely known that the individual who wrote the epistle of Acts is Luke, who also penned the Gospel of Luke. Therefore, we know that during this time of Paul's travel, a brother in Christ, namely Luke, was with him. Yet, this missionary travel that Paul is on in Acts 21 is a continuation of travel from what is seen in Acts 20, and as we look at Acts 20, we not only see Luke with Paul indicated by the usage of the terms **"us"** and **"we"** in Acts 20:5-6, but we also see seven additional men with Paul and Luke, as we look at Acts 20:4-6 KJV:

"And there accompanied him into Asia Sopater of Berea; and of the Thessalonians, Aristarchus and Secundus; and Gaius of Derbe, and Timotheus; and of Asia, Tychicus and Trophimus. These going before tarried for us at Troas. And we sailed away from Philippi after the days of unleavened bread, and came unto them to Troas in five days; where we abode seven days."

This travel that began with Paul and his companions in Acts 20:4 is a total of at least nine men. As they are going through various regions on Paul's way to Jerusalem (Acts 20:16), it is the same travel that Paul and his companions are on as they enter Philip's house in Acts 21:8. Now that these facts have been established, there are two points that we shall address. First, as Paul and his companions are traveling through various locations, Paul makes a statement to the elders at Ephesus that he was previously told that bonds and afflictions await him in Jerusalem (Acts 20:22-23). However, Paul said it was the Holy Spirit testifying to this fact in every city. As we realize that prophets and prophetesses speak by the authority of God, Paul confirms in Acts 20:23 that it is the Holy Spirit who gives them the word. The word that was given to Paul in every city was teaching Paul what was going to happen to him in Jerusalem. Thus, the individuals who were teaching this information to Paul about what awaits him in Jerusalem had the authority to teach Paul, who was also with at least eight other men in his travels. As we look at the commands in 1 Corinthians 14:34 and 1 Timothy 2:11-15, we know that the individuals who taught Paul this information in every city he was in were prophets and not prophetesses. As there was authority in not specifically teaching Paul alone, but also the men with him were also being taught this information, thereby giving the individuals who spoke of the bonds and afflictions awaiting

Paul the authority to teach multiple men in one setting the word of God. This much is seen in Acts 21:4-5 KJV:

"And finding disciples, we tarried there seven days: who said to Paul through the Spirit, that he should not go up to Jerusalem. And when we had accomplished those days, we departed and went our way; and they all brought us on our way, with wives and children, till we were out of the city: and we kneeled down on the shore, and prayed."

It is confirmed that the disciples in Acts 21:4 *"who said to Paul through the Spirit, that he should not go up to Jerusalem"* were men, by what is said of all the disciples in Acts 21:5 *"they all brought us on our way, with wives and children."* All the disciples had wives and children, thus confirming that the prophetic word being spoken to Paul and the men of whom Paul is among, instructing Paul not to go to Jerusalem, were men.

Second, in Acts 21:8-9, as the total of nine Christian men enter the house of Philip, who also *"had four daughters, virgins, which did prophesy,"* we notice a limitation of teaching placed on these four prophetesses; as they lack the authority from God to teach Paul and his traveling companions what will happen to Paul in Jerusalem. Unlike the disciples in Acts 21:4 who had the authority to instruct Paul through the Spirit not to go to Jerusalem while he and his travel companions were in their presence, the four daughters of Philip were not given that authority to do the same nor to teach him what was to happen to him in Jerusalem. This much is known by the two verses immediately following Acts 21:9, as it is seen in Acts 21:10-11 KJV:

"And as we tarried there many days, there came down from Judaea a certain prophet, named Agabus. And when he was come unto us, he took Paul's girdle, and bound his own hands and feet, and said, Thus saith the Holy Ghost, So shall the Jews at Jerusalem bind the man

that owneth this girdle, and shall deliver him into the hands of the Gentiles."

Even though Paul and his travel companions (a total of nine men) were in the presence of four prophetesses, it is the prophet Agabus who is given the authority from God for the Holy Spirit to testify through what will happen to Paul in Jerusalem. Agabus not only taught this information to Paul, but the setting also included all of Paul's travel companions and a company of people in the place where they were located. As seen in Acts 21:12 KJV:

"And when we heard these things, both we, and they of that place, besought him not to go up to Jerusalem."

Here it is confirmed by the writer Luke that he, the rest of Paul's travel companions, and *"they of that place"* besought Paul *"not to go to Jerusalem."* A teaching instructing Paul about what will happen to him, while at the same time teaching several men in Paul's travel companions and a group of people who are also in their midst at the same time, as they all urged Paul not to go. Thus, making the instruction coming from the prophet Agabus a public teaching of God; even though there were four prophetesses in their presence, God did not give any of those four the authority to teach these men and those in that place what would happen to Paul. The company of nine, including Paul and the multiple people of the locale they were in, made the teaching public. Philip's four daughters were plainly restricted from this ability by the authority of God being given to the prophet Agabus in the very next verse.

The authority given to the disciples in Acts 21:4-5 to instruct Paul through the Spirit, with the restriction seen in the four daughters of Philip who prophesied not having the authority to teach Paul and his travel companions, yet given to Agabus in the very next verses in Acts 21:8-12 by God, confirms the implementation of God by what is said in 1 Corinthians 14:34 and 1 Timothy 2:11-15.

7

The Patriarchal Age

Our study of the previously mentioned authority/subjection law now brings us to the very beginning of the scriptures with the Patriarchal Age. As Paul stated in 1 Corinthians 14:34, *"as also saith the law"*, and then fully explained in his letter to Timothy in 1 Timothy 2:11-14 KJV, *"Let the woman learn in silence with all subjection. But I suffer not a woman to teach, nor to usurp authority over the man, but to be in silence. For Adam was first formed, then Eve. And Adam was not deceived, but the woman being deceived was in the transgression."* As we continue to show that this specific law, which has not changed from the beginning, is inclusive of all public platforms, it's imperative to know that based on how the law has been implemented from the beginning, any other way of interpreting or implementing this law does not meet the standard of the law in question. We now examine God's direct communication with Adam and Eve in the book of Genesis and how God implements this specific law from the very beginning, in the Patriarchal Age and the Mosaic Age. The scriptures tell us in Genesis 2:15-16 KJV:

"And the Lord God took the man and put him into the garden of

Eden to dress it and to keep it. And the Lord God commanded the man, saying, of every tree of the garden thou mayest freely eat, but of the tree of the knowledge of good and evil, thou shalt not eat of it, for in the day that thou eatest thereof thou shalt surely die."

From this, we see in the beginning that God created Adam first, put him in the garden to work, and gave him a command stemming from a law that God specifically had at this time for man. Just as Paul stated in 1 Timothy 2:13 KJV *"For Adam was first formed then Eve."* What we see in Genesis 2:15-17 is that man was given law before the creation of Eve. As we further look at Genesis 2, specifically in verse 18, we find the mention of God creating a help meet for Adam: *"And the Lord God said, it is not good that man should be alone; I will make him an help meet for him."* We know this is Eve, as Genesis 2:21-23 KJV tells us:

"And the Lord God caused a deep sleep to fall upon Adam, and he slept: and he took one of his ribs, and closed up the flesh instead thereof; And the rib, which the Lord God had taken from man, made he a woman, and brought her unto the man. And Adam said, this is now bone of my bones, and flesh of my flesh: she shall be called Woman, because she was taken out of Man."

As we notice from this set of scriptures in Genesis, when compared with the statements the apostle Paul makes in 1 Corinthians 14:34 and 1 Timothy 2:11-14, God is explaining to us what the law is from the very beginning. Yet we still have one more reason as to why this law has been active from the beginning: 1 Timothy 2:14 KJV:

"And Adam was not deceived, but the woman being deceived was in the transgression."

When we look at Genesis chapter 3, we see the devil, known as a murderer from the beginning and the father of lies by Jesus (John 8:44), tempting Eve to break God's command for mankind. Eve and Adam broke God's command and ate of the tree of knowledge of good and evil, as stated in Genesis 3:6 KJV:

"And when the woman saw that the tree was good for food, and that it was pleasant to the eyes, and a tree to be desired to make one wise, she took of the fruit thereof, and did eat, and gave also unto her husband with her; and he did eat."

Once Adam and Eve ate the fruit, Genesis 3:7 tells us:

"And the eyes of them both were opened, and they knew that they were naked; and they sewed fig leaves together and made themselves aprons."

What Adam and Eve did was a public act of disobedience in the garden of Eden. Here are some imperative facts: These sinful actions involved the whole of the human race at this time, which is what made this public sin. The fact that God created and gave spiritual teaching to Adam before Eve was created implies that Adam had the created responsibility to teach his wife. Additionally, as we consider the authority/subjection law stated by the apostle Paul, based on this historical account, the necessary inference (irresistible truth) concludes this law entails all public teaching, as Adam was the public authority of the world tasked with teaching his wife, Eve. Since the law involved all public teaching during the time of Adam, the authority/subjection law stated by the apostle Paul transcends cultural barriers, going back to the beginning, and confirms this law entails all public teaching as it pertains to the gospel of Christ as well.

Continuing in Genesis 3, after they have committed this sinful act, they hear the voice of God in the garden. Look at who God addresses first, as stated in Genesis 3:9: *"And the Lord God called unto Adam, and said unto him, Where art thou?"* This further concludes that Adam being created first is the reason why God addresses Adam first. With this consideration, we see that God Himself has from the very beginning followed this law in how He addresses the human race. Additionally, we see as a result of Eve *"being deceived and, in the transgression"* (1 Timothy 2:14), God makes a statement to her in Genesis 3:16 KJV:

"Unto the woman he said, I will greatly multiply thy sorrow and thy conception; in sorrow thou shalt bring forth children; and thy desire shall be to thy husband, and he shall rule over thee."

Of particular interest in this passage is the Hebrew word for "rule," which is **mashal;** it means to make to have dominion, governor, rule, or have power. This word is used 81 times in 74 verses throughout the Old Testament, and each time this word is used, it refers to what is known publicly. All 74 verses with this word are cited in the Appendix for your examination.

As we continue to look at the scriptural implementation of the authority/subjection law in the Patriarchal Age, let us continue to examine how God shows by example in Genesis chapter 4 the execution of this law, which transpires from the events in Genesis chapters 2-3. I now call your attention to Cain and Abel in Genesis 4:3-4 KJV:

"And in process of time it came to pass, that Cain brought of the fruit of the ground an offering unto the Lord. And Abel, he also brought of the firstlings of his flock and of the fat thereof. And the Lord had respect unto Abel and to his offering."

Two things worthy of note as we look at the account of Cain and Abel: First, we see that both Cain and Abel offered worship to God; however, only Abel's offering was accepted. While there were women at this time, referenced by the fact that Cain knew his wife and she conceived

in Genesis 4:17 KJV:
"And Cain knew his wife; and she conceived, and bare Enoch."

We see that the men had the responsibility of leading the worship that God requested at this time. The second thing worthy of note is that the scriptures tell us that Abel was a prophet. As we look at the words of Jesus in Luke 11:50-51 KJV:
"That the blood of all the prophets, which was shed from the foundation of the world, may be required of this generation; From the blood of Abel unto the blood of Zacharias which perished between the altar and the temple: verily I say unto you, It shall be required of this generation."

A prophet was one whom God spoke to, a foreteller and speaker of God's word to man. One who denounced the sins of the people and called for repentance of their sins. Abel is described as a prophet in the same way that all the prophets of God were known, all the way to Zechariah. The reason why Abel's sacrifice was acceptable to God and Cain's was unacceptable is that God told both Cain and Abel what sacrifice to give to Him. This is evident in the following verses: Hebrews 11:4 KJV:
"By faith Abel offered unto God a more excellent sacrifice than Cain, by which he obtained witness that he was righteous, God testifying of his gifts: and by it he being dead yet speaketh."

And Romans 10:17 KJV:
"So then faith cometh by hearing, and hearing by the word of God."

With the scriptures holding the authority/subjection law in view from the beginning, we see God following this law in addressing the men to lead the worship to Himself in offering sacrifices. The scriptures tell us pertaining to Abel as a prophet that from the beginning, God gave His word specifically to the men to speak publicly on His behalf **(implementing the authority/subjection law Paul mentioned in 1 Corinthians 14:34 and 1 Timothy 2:11-14)**; giving public instruction on how man is to be in right standing with Him. In Genesis 4:8 KJV, the scriptures tell us:

"And Cain talked with Abel his brother: and it came to pass, when they were in the field, that Cain rose up against Abel his brother and slew him."

We then see that God cursed Cain for this sinful act: Genesis 4:11 KJV:

"And now thou art cursed from the earth, which hath opened her mouth to receive thy brother's blood from thy hand."

In the verses following Genesis 4:11, there are some interesting facts to address; particularly Genesis 4:17-23 KJV:

"And Cain knew his wife; and she conceived, and bare Enoch: and he builded a city, and called the name of the city, after the name of his son, Enoch. And unto Enoch was born Irad: and Irad begat Mehujael: and Mehujael begat Methusael: and Methusael begat Lamech. And Lamech took unto him two wives: the name of the one was Adah, and the name of the other Zillah. And Adah bare Jabal: he was the father of such as dwell in tents, and of such as have cattle. And his brother's name was Jubal: he was the father of all such as handle the harp and organ. And Zillah, she also bare Tubalcain, an instructor of every artificer in brass and iron: and the sister of Tubalcain was Naamah .And Lamech said unto his wives, Adah and Zillah, hear my voice; ye wives of Lamech, hearken unto my speech: for I have slain a man to my wounding, and a young man to my hurt."

Here are the following facts to mention about these verses. By naming the patriarchs, God is placing emphasis on the male as the authority figure in society (**every aspect of public affairs**), following the authority/subjection law from the beginning. We see that the males were the authority figures in society, as evidenced by the fact that they built cities, were the fathers of those who dwelt in tents, and were instructors in making bronze and iron.

Additionally, with Lamech, even though his situation was sinful, as he was a polygamist (having two wives), we see the women in this situation understanding that Lamech, being the male, was the authority figure. Hence, they were subject to him as their husband, and he spoke with authority to them as he arrogantly explained his sinful actions of murder.

This further evidences that the authority/subjection law was publicly known and observed by all in their cultural society, albeit not in observance of God. It is not until Genesis 4:26, with the birth of Seth's son Enos, that men began to call on the name of the Lord, as it reads:
"And to Seth, to him also there was born a son; and he called his name Enos: then began men to call on the name of the Lord."

The emphasis on "men" is due to their responsibility under what we've addressed as the authority/subjection law. With that said; what does it mean to call on the name of the Lord? Calling on the name of the Lord means a person is conducting themselves by the authority of God or with God's approval; the name of the Lord is His authority. For a scriptural example, I briefly call your attention to Acts 4:7-10 KJV for a response by the apostle Peter when he was asked by what power or name he healed a man, as it states:
"And when they had set them in the midst, they asked, by what power, or by what name, have ye done this? Then Peter, filled with the Holy

Ghost, said unto them, Ye rulers of the people, and elders of Israel, If we this day be examined of the good deed done to the impotent man, by what means he is made whole; Be it known unto you all, and to all the people of Israel, that by the name of Jesus Christ of Nazareth, whom ye crucified, whom God raised from the dead, even by him doth this man stand here before you whole."

When Annas the high priest, Caiaphas, John, Alexander, and as many as were kindred of the high priest asked Peter this question in Acts 4:7, Peter stated it was by the name of Jesus Christ (by His authority). As we return to Genesis 4:26, to call on the name of the Lord is to appeal to the Lord's authority. It must also be understood that calling on the name of the Lord involves more than just worship in this verse. As we've discussed, Cain and Abel were told by God what offering to give to Him in worship back in Genesis 4:4-5. Calling on the name of the Lord involved a person's conduct of living, giving the specific worship God requested, and speaking publicly by the authority of the Lord, with God's approval to speak on His behalf to man. Prior to the birth of Enos, there was not a lineage of men inclusive of the public space as a whole in society who publicly worshiped God nor spoke publicly with His approval and authority. As we pay close attention to these scriptures, let us once again see the way that God implements His authority/subjection law through the men in the public sphere.

Looking at Genesis chapters 5-6:2, these men in the lineage of Enos had many sons and daughters. For example, I call your attention to Genesis 5:9-11 KJV:

"And Enos lived ninety years, and begat Cainan: And Enos lived after he begat Cainan eight hundred and fifteen years, and begat sons and daughters: And all the days of Enos were nine hundred and five years: and he died."

This is seen with each man named in his lineage in Genesis chapter 5. Yet the authority of both leading public worship and speaking publicly on behalf of God was specifically tasked to the men, as referenced in Genesis 4:26 KJV:

"Then began men to call on the name of the Lord."

A critical fact to understand as we acknowledge calling on the name of the Lord means what's done in the Lord's name is with the authority and approval of God. Looking at Paul's statements in 1 Corinthians 14:34 KJV:

"Let your women keep silence in the churches: for it is not permitted unto them to speak; but they are commanded to be under obedience as also saith the law."

And in 1 Timothy 2:12 KJV:

"But I suffer not a woman to teach nor usurp authority over the man but to be in silence. For Adam was first formed, then Eve And Adam was not deceived, but the woman being deceived was in the transgression."

This authority/subjection law was clearly implemented in the beginning, as we look at the book of Genesis. Prior to the establishment of the church and before God chose a nation, this law was inclusive of all public arenas within the world's population. Therefore, since Paul is using and confirming this standard of what the church operates by, the necessary inference (irresistible truth) entails that the same is to be abided by all in the Lord's church. Furthermore, there are two men that stand out in the lineage of Enos in Genesis chapter 5 that I would like to call your attention to. The first person for our consideration is the son of Jared, whose name is Enoch, as stated in Genesis 5:18 KJV:

"And Jared lived an hundred sixty and two years, and he begat

Enoch."

Enoch stands out here in chapter 5 not only because the scriptures tell us in Genesis 5:24 KJV: that *"Enoch walked with God, and he was not, for God took him."* Yes, Enoch was one who pleased God so much that he was blessed in not having to see death, being one of only two individuals ever to experience being translated without physically dying; the other being the prophet Elijah (2 Kings 2). But Enoch also stands out here because he was a prophet of God, as the scriptures also confirm this about him in Jude vv. 14-15 KJV:

"And Enoch also, the seventh from Adam, prophesied of these, saying, Behold, the Lord cometh with ten thousands of his saints, To execute judgment upon all, and to convince all that are ungodly among them of all their ungodly deeds which they have ungodly committed, and of all their hard speeches which ungodly sinners have spoken against him."

As we look at this prophecy that Enoch proclaimed of the Lord, there are a few things worthy of mentioning. First, Enoch is speaking on behalf of the Lord, publicly convicting all that are ungodly; prior to the worship assembly and prior to the choosing of a nation; Enoch spoke on behalf of the Lord to **all**; this thereby acknowledges that the entire public platform is under consideration as we look at the authority/subjection law that the inspired apostle Paul says is from the beginning. We see that this is how God implemented this law in the beginning, which He confirms is not to be changed, even under the gospel of Christ. The second observation we make, confirming Enoch was a prophet according to Jude vv. 14-15, as we align this with what is said about the lineage of men who called on the name of the Lord in Genesis 4:26-6:2, is that according to Genesis 6:2 KJV:

"That the sons of God saw the daughters of men that they were fair;

and they took them wives of all which they chose."

These men were known as the sons of God. Therefore, these men who called on the name of the Lord in the lineage of Enos, who were known as sons of God, were also prophets, just as Enoch was a prophet. As we have confirmed, with the specific mentioning of these men in Genesis 5, even though they had sons and daughters, it confirms the role of teaching the word of God in the public sphere of men and women, as implemented in the beginning by God's unchanging law given to man. Our third and last observation, as we look at the prophet Enoch, is that though he is no longer on this side of eternity, Enoch is still teaching men and women today on the same public platform he did before God took him, known as the worldwide platform. As individuals pick up the word of God and read and study Enoch's prophecy in Jude vv. 14-15 and how he walked with God in Genesis 5:22-24, we see the unchanging authority/subjection law still implemented among all today. Enoch's bold public proclamations still speak on behalf of the Lord through his words found in these scriptures.

The second man that I would like to call your attention to is Noah. We first hear of Noah in Genesis 5:28-32 KJV:

"And Lamech lived an hundred eighty and two years, and begat a son and he called his name Noah, saying, this same shall comfort us concerning our work and toil of our hands, because of the ground which the Lord hath cursed. And Lamech lived after he begat Noah five hundred ninety and five years, and begat sons and daughters and all the days of Lamech were seven hundred seventy and seven years: and he died. And Noah was five hundred years old: and Noah begat Shem, Ham, and Japheth."

Noah, in like manner to his great-grandfather Enoch, was a man known as a son of God, one who called on the name of the Lord, and a man known by God as one who walked with God, righteous and blameless in his generation, as stated in Genesis 6:9 KJV:

"These are the generations of Noah: Noah was a just man and perfect in his generations, and Noah walked with God."

Additionally, Noah was a prophet to the world at a time when God was bringing destruction upon the entirety of the human race. As we notice with the law from the beginning, the emphasis is on man leading and speaking with God's approval and authority in every facet of the public sphere as God has implemented. Noah is by far the most significant example in the Patriarchal Age as he preached to the entire world. In a time when God was sorry that He made man on the earth because of the wickedness of man being great on the earth, a time when God saw that every imagination of the thoughts of his heart was continually on evil, as stated in Genesis 6:5-6 KJV:

"And God saw that the wickedness of man was great in the earth, and that every imagination of the thoughts of his heart was only evil continually. And it repented the Lord that he had made man on the earth, and it grieved him at his heart."

But *"Noah found grace in the eyes of the Lord"* (Genesis 6:8 KJV). What is interesting to note about Noah is that not only does God tell Noah to build an ark with specific details in how the ark was to be built, as stated in Genesis 6:13-16 KJV:

"And God said unto Noah, The end of all flesh is come before me; for the earth is filled with violence through them; and, behold, I will destroy them with the earth. Make thee an ark of gopher wood; rooms shalt thou make in the ark, and shalt pitch it within and without with pitch. And this is the fashion which thou shalt make it of: The length of the ark shall be three hundred cubits, the breadth of it fifty cubits,

and the height of it thirty cubits. A window shalt thou make to the ark, and in a cubit shalt thou finish it above; and the door of the ark shalt thou set in the side thereof; with lower, second, and third stories shalt thou make it."

But also, Noah was a preacher of righteousness. There are two sets of verses that are imperative to the argument at hand, found in the New Testament spoken by the apostle Peter. The first set of scripture that I call to your attention is found in 2 Peter 2:5 KJV:

"And spared not the old world, but saved Noah the eighth person, a preacher of righteousness, bringing in the flood upon the world of the ungodly."

In understanding the public platform to be inclusive of all aspects of the public arena and the preaching that Noah did, as we note God's implementation of the authority/subjection law, we must understand the overwhelming effects of the flood upon the world of the ungodly. Was this flood confined to a region or locale in its destruction, or was this literally a global flood? The scriptural evidence lets us know that this flood was absolutely a global flood. Consider what the apostle Peter furthermore tells us in 2 Peter 3:5-6 KJV:

"For this they willingly are ignorant of, that by the word of God the heavens were of old, and the earth standing out of the water and in the water Whereby the world that then was, being overflowed with water, perished."

Peter tells us that the world of Noah's day and time during the flood was overflowed with water and perished. Additionally, we find this statement made in Genesis 7:18-20 KJV:

"And the waters prevailed and were increased greatly upon the earth; and the ark went upon the face of the waters. And the waters prevailed

exceedingly upon the earth; and all the high hills, that were under the whole heaven, were covered. Fifteen cubits upward did the waters prevail; and the mountains were covered."

All the high hills and mountains under the whole heaven were covered. This lets us know that, as Noah was a preacher of righteousness on behalf of the Lord, he preached to the entire world of the ungodly, inclusive of all aspects of public preaching available to him during God's patiently waiting time for repentance of 120 years (Genesis 6:3).

The second set of scriptures that I call your attention to is found in 1 Peter 3:18-20 KJV:

"For Christ also hath once suffered for sins, the just for the unjust, that he might bring us to God, being put to death in the flesh, but quickened by the Spirit by which also he went and preached unto the spirits in prison Which sometime were disobedient, when once the longsuffering of God waited in the days of Noah, while the ark was a preparing, wherein few, that is, eight souls were saved by water."

Now that we know the flood brought in by God was a worldwide flood, destroying all but eight souls, we now see in Peter's first epistle that the Spirit of Christ preached to those souls of Noah's day, who are now in prison—a sobering thought indeed. One may ask how the Spirit of Christ preached to those souls during Noah's day and why they are now in prison. Keep in mind, men began to call on the name of the Lord with the lineage of Enos; this includes the public teaching with the authority and approval of God. Noah, a prophet of the lineage of Enos, one whom God spoke to, and a preacher of God's righteousness, spoke with the Spirit of Christ in him, as stated about the prophets in 1 Peter 1:10-11 KJV:

"Concerning this salvation, the prophets who prophesied about the

grace that was to be yours searched and inquired carefully, inquiring what person or time the Spirit of Christ in them was indicating when he predicted the sufferings of Christ and the subsequent glories."

Every soul in the entire world during Noah's time had the opportunity to repent through Noah's preaching while God patiently waited at that time. The public speaking on behalf of God was given to a man, though four of the saved souls in the old world were women. By Noah preaching the righteousness of God and teaching man to repent of their ungodly ways, he was able to use all public platforms available to him in teaching the entire world to return to Godly living in the sight of the Lord; further evidence that God implemented His authority/subjection law to include all public platforms of speaking with God's approval and authority.

Lastly, as pertaining to Noah and his sons after the floodwaters receded, I call your attention to whom God addresses when giving His commands, which is found in Genesis 9:1 KJV:

"And God blessed Noah and his sons and said to them, "Be fruitful and multiply and fill the earth."

And again, in Genesis 9:3-6 KJV:

"Every moving thing that lives shall be food for you. And as I gave you the green plants, I give you everything. But you shall not eat flesh with its life, that is, its blood. And for your lifeblood I will require a reckoning: from every beast I will require it and from man. From his fellow man I will require a reckoning for the life of man. Whoever sheds the blood of man, by man shall his blood be shed, for God made man in his own image."

When God is now ready to repopulate the world, He specifically addresses and gives His commands to the men—Noah and his sons. God has given these men the responsibility of teaching His commands to the entire world with His authority and approval. God implements the authority/subjection law in repopulating the world the same way He did in the beginning when He created the world with Adam and Eve. What Paul stated in 1 Corinthians 14:34 and 1 Timothy 2:11-14 falls in line with what we see in the very beginning with the Patriarchs. The way God implemented this law in the beginning encompassed every avenue of the public platform, since this is what the apostle Paul appeals to in the New Testament under the gospel of Christ, alerts us that no change is to be had at all. The rest of the book of Genesis holds the pattern of the authority/subjection law we see here in the beginning, with no changes. From the nations descending from Noah in Genesis chapter 10 to Joseph ruling over Egypt in Genesis chapter 50, God's implementation of 1 Corinthians 14:34 KJV: *"as also saith the law"* and 1 Timothy 2:11-14 KJV: *"Let the woman learn in silence with all subjection. But I suffer not a woman to teach, nor to usurp authority over the man, but to be in silence. For Adam was first formed, then Eve. And Adam was not deceived, but the woman being deceived was in the transgression."* is seen throughout the entire book. We will now move into the Law of Moses as we continue to discuss the scriptural implementation of the authority/subjection law.

8

The Law of Moses

The account of the Law of Moses begins in the book of Exodus, yet it stems from the emphasis placed on one specific family in the book of Genesis: Abraham, Isaac, and Jacob. As we look at this family, we see that the choosing of Abraham was intentional—not by means of specifically selecting Abraham for the Messiah to come through, but by means of following the law that was established in the beginning. What is meant by intentional is that God has a specific plan designed to carry out His desired outcome and achieve His goal. His goal is always implemented by the word He has spoken. To know what God means by His law, we must look not only at the individuals He selected to speak for Him but also at His perspective on the intention of influence He wants His representatives to have on the whole of mankind. God chose Abraham to be the father of a nation, a nation that was to be known by the entire world as God's chosen people—a people led by the example of one man's obedience to God, who also was a prophet of God. Genesis 20:7 KJV:

"Now therefore restore the man his wife; for he is a prophet, and he shall pray for thee, and thou shalt live: and if thou restore her not,

know thou that thou shalt surely die, thou, and all that are thine."

As we see according to the Scriptures, Abraham was a prophet. This is consistent with the other prophets we previously discussed, who called on the name of the Lord. Two verses concerning Abraham that confirm this are Genesis 12:8 KJV:

"And he removed from thence unto a mountain on the east of Bethel, and pitched his tent, having Bethel on the west, and Hai on the east: and there he built an altar unto the Lord, and called upon the name of the Lord."

And Genesis 13:4 KJV:

"Unto the place of the altar, which he had make there at the first: and there Abram called on the name of the Lord."

With this information in mind, here are some indisputable facts. God specifically chose the male Abraham, keeping to the authority/subjection law He gave in the beginning with Genesis 3:16. Because He chose Abraham according to this law to be the father of a physical, fleshly nation for the world to acknowledge and spiritually to all who believe in Christ, God's implementation of this law through Abraham shows that His intention for this law is inclusive of every public avenue teaching the human race about God. I call your attention to Romans 4:13 KJV:

"For the promise, that he should be the heir of the world, was not to Abraham, or to his seed, through the law, but through the righteousness of faith."

As Paul has mentioned the example of Abraham in the epistle to the Romans, describing how one is justified in Christ, anyone who desires to be justified by God through Jesus Christ must emulate the example of Abraham, which preceded the law of Moses. With that said, the specific statement in this verse we will address is *"For the promise that he should be the heir of the world."*

The first thing to mention about this statement is that it explains the reasoning behind the last statement made in Romans 4:12 by the Greek primary particle *"Gar"*. What is said in verse 12 is:

"And the father of circumcision to them who are not of the circumcision only, but who also walk in the steps of that faith of our father Abraham, which he had being yet uncircumcised."

Why this is critical to the topic at hand is that we see God implementing the authority/subjection law by having a male lead as the example for the entire world to be in right standing with God. With emphasis on the heir of the world, God has not only implemented His authority/subjection law but additionally shows us how inclusive this law is to the male leading in every place; as the world is the ultimate public platform from which the man Abraham is to be looked to by all in the world, as God's example of belief as righteousness. God, following His authority/subjection law from the beginning by selecting a man to be heir in every place through Abraham, implements the example for the entire world. What the Scriptures have us to know about Abraham is stated in Genesis 26:3-5 KJV:

"Sojourn in this land, and I will be with thee, and will bless thee; for unto thee, and unto thy seed, I will give all these countries, and I will perform the oath which I sware unto Abraham thy father; and I will make thy seed to multiply as the stars of heaven, and will give unto thy seed all these countries; and in thy seed shall all the nations of the earth be blessed; because that Abraham obeyed my voice, and kept my charge, my commandments, my statutes, and my laws."

When the world was to look at the nation of Israel and its physical founding father, this is what the public was to be taught: that God selected this man to be a father of a nation because he obeyed God. And this was intentionally implemented by God. Heir of the world definitively means one who receives his allotted possession by right of sonship. This not only applies to Abraham, but this also applies to multitudes of people in the world who faithfully obey our risen Lord and Savior Jesus Christ, who is the seed of Abraham; crossing cultural barriers, time zones, continents, and languages. Looking at God's choice of the male for this purpose confirms that this was done in accordance with what Paul stated in 1 Corinthians 14:34 *"as also saith the law"*, of which we have methodically examined in Genesis. According to what the word of God says in Romans 4:23-24, the platform of publishing God's word through the written format was done not just for Abraham's sake but for all who believe in Him who raised Jesus our Lord from the dead. Romans 4:23-24 KJV:

"Now it was not written for his sake alone that it was imputed to him, but also for us. It shall be imputed to us who believe in Him who raised up Jesus our Lord from the dead."

There are different platforms of public teaching, and this is an example of one: the availability of the scriptures to an audience inclusive of the whole world, the written word in the form of epistles or letters, and these were to be published to the world, which by definition means to make public. Consider these two sets of verses, out of many, which confirm the necessity and urgency of this truth about God's word. 2 Timothy 3:15-17 KJV:

"And that from a child thou hast known the holy scriptures, which are able to make thee wise unto salvation through faith which is in Christ Jesus. All scripture is given by inspiration of God, and is profitable for doctrine, for reproof, for correction, for instruction in righteousness:

That the man of God may be perfect, thoroughly furnished unto all good works."

The apostle Paul, who wrote nearly half of the New Testament, confirms that all scripture is God-breathed and leads to salvation through faith in Jesus Christ. This alerts us to the fact that if there is any individual in the world who desires salvation, that individual must first have the inspired word of God and then come to obedient faith in the inspired word of God. This means there is a necessity to have God's word, the holy scriptures, published to the entire world. We see this to be true by the scripture we have in Romans 4:13, in which Abraham is "heir of the world"; because this statement includes the whole world, the whole world must have this information. The second set of verses that I call your attention to is found in the gospel of John 12:46-49 KJV:

"I am come a light into the world, that whosoever believeth on me should not abide in darkness. And if any man hear my words, and believe not, I judge him not: for I came not to judge the world, but to save the world. He that rejecteth me, and receiveth not my words, hath one that judgeth him: the word that I have spoken, the same shall judge him in the last day. For I have not spoken of myself; but the Father which sent me, He gave me a commandment, what I should say, and what I should speak."

Because all scripture is given by inspiration of God, which means the scriptures come directly from God Himself and He is going to judge the world through His word, it confirms the urgency of the scriptures being extended to the world for the opportunity for salvation for all. What we see from these examples is that God, in following His authority/subjection law, has used men by the method of written publishing (making public) His word to spread to the entire world. The early methods that were used to convey God's word to a multitude of people outside of verbal preaching were scrolls. What has replaced the scrolls and has become the most popular method to publish God's word since is the codex format, which stacks the scriptures in the style of pages that are typically bound at the left edge. This is what we call books today, and namely, as it pertains to the scriptures, what we call The Bible. This alerts us to the extent and nature of the authority/subjection law because it encompasses a lane of public teaching different from the lane of verbal preaching and teaching, by way of written rather than spoken. When there is written teaching available to multitudes of people, transcending time, continents, cultures, and language barriers at one time (which the scriptures do), the platform is public. This is why we only see male writers of the scriptures, as it is a public platform.

An additional example is also seen in Abel, as scripture teaches us in Hebrews 11:4 KJV:
"he being dead yet speaketh."

His example of faith publicly speaks to everyone in the world, saved and unsaved alike, teaching through the method of the published written word of God, which denotes a medium of preaching and teaching God's word (***2 Thessalonians 1:7-8***).

The Example For Modern Media

However, there are three other avenues of public teaching that are equal to the worldwide platform of the method of the published scriptures (the Bible); all of which come from the realm of public media broadcasting: radio, social media, and television broadcasting. Like the worldwide audience that the scriptures have through the method of written teaching of God's word, of which Abraham is the example to the world by being "heir of the world," the realm of public media broadcasting reaches multitudes of people, transcending time, continents, culture, and language, all at the same time verbally (through spoken words). What we see in the written format and the public media broadcasting format are equal mediums used to convey the same message. Though the medium is different, they produce the same effect; this is a method often known as inter-method reliability because of the equal outcome they produce. Public media broadcasting, being the newer method of the 21st century, has the same effect, measure, and value as the established method God used in publishing His word through the medium of the published scroll and book on the worldwide platform. Because the mentioned avenues in public media broadcasting are equal to the avenue of book publishing in spreading God's word, transcending cultural and continental boundaries and reaching multitudes at once, the same standard in God's unchanging authority/subjection law applies.

In continuing with our example of Abraham and the authority/subjection law, we must examine if it follows the pattern that God has implemented with this law with the men who came before Abraham, which we addressed in Genesis chapters 1-11. What we see is the same selecting of a male to speak and prophesy publicly with the authority of God in calling on the name of the Lord in Abraham as in the previous examples. I call your attention to Genesis 12:8 KJV:

"And he removed from thence unto a mountain on the east of Bethel, and pitched his tent, having Bethel on the west, and Hai on the east: and there he builded an altar unto the Lord, and called upon the name of the Lord."

And Genesis 13:4 KJV:

"Unto the place of the altar, which he had make there at the first: and there Abram called on the name of the Lord."

These verses, along with the statement that God made stating that Abraham was a prophet, factually show us that this is what God implemented and intended for His authority/subjection law to cover.

Here are some undeniable facts with the example of Abraham, given in Romans 4:13 being "heir of the world." His example is known to us solely through scripture, which we must follow if we desire to be justified by God, submitting ourselves to His word. As this equates to Paul's statements in 1 Corinthians 14:34 KJV:

"Let your women keep silence in the churches: for it is not permitted unto them to speak; but they are commanded to be under obedience as also saith the law."

And 1 Timothy 2:11-14 KJV:

"Let the woman learn in silence with all subjection. But I suffer not a woman to teach, nor to usurp authority over the man, but to be in silence. For Adam was first formed, then Eve. And Adam was not deceived, but the woman being deceived was in the transgression."

It is to be acknowledged that since Paul based this statement on preexisting law that was established in the beginning, and this law was implemented by God on public platforms before the church assembly and outside of the church assembly, as evident in the example of Abraham leading the way for the entire world as he is known as "heir of the world," it concludes that the authority/subjection law is not limited specifically to the assembly of worship but is inclusive of all public teaching to be done with the approval and authority from God. This is how God implemented this law prior to the church, of which Paul says still stands by his statement of *"as also saith the law,"* making what is to be done in the Lord's church equal to how God implemented this law before the establishment of the Lord's church. Whether the well-established medium of published writing to multitudes (which God implemented through inspired writers) or the new medium of public media broadcasting to multitudes, they produce exactly the same effect in conveying God's unchanging word. And what He has decreed by Scriptural Implementation is what we find both in 1 Corinthians 14:34 and 1 Timothy 2:11-14. Because Abraham is the heir of the world and God specifically sought out the male for public authority, public leading, and public example, we continue to see this intentionality that God uses with the establishment of His covenant with the promise that God made to Abraham, as noted in Genesis 17:1-3 KJV:

"When Abram was ninety-nine years old, the Lord appeared to Abram and said to him, I am Almighty God; walk before Me and be blameless. And I will make My covenant between Me and you and will multiply you exceedingly. Then Abram fell on his face, and God talked with him, saying: As for Me, behold, My covenant is with you, and you shall be a father of many nations."

Scriptural covenants are public records that the world has access to. Whoever God chose to establish His covenant with was to publicly lead the way for multitudes of people to choose whether to be in a covenant relationship with God, with the example being the faithfulness of the one whom God chose to establish His covenant with (Abraham). From the very beginning in Genesis up to this point with Abraham, what we see from God is a firm decision to use the male publicly in relaying His will for all mankind; God shows a resolution on a course of action that has not wavered in who He has sought out to have His approval to act publicly on His behalf. The determined resolve in specifically choosing the male for public leading, additionally displayed by the lack of intention to use the female in these public settings, shows how God is implementing the authority/subjection law of which Paul discusses in 1 Corinthians 14:34 and 1 Timothy 2:8-15. Of critical importance as well is the fact that God had not yet set up the law requirements for the assembling for worship to Him, yet He has made a clear determined choice in who has His approval to speak and lead on the public platform on His behalf. And as we are examining the statement *"as also saith the law"*, and this law is clearly defined in 1 Timothy 2:11-15, this example further shows how God implements this law, extending beyond the boundaries of assembling for worship and inclusive of the entire public platform. When we see God intentionally resolute with the firm decision to publicly use the male in every instance with the lack of intention to use the female in the same instance from the very beginning, the necessary inference shows that God is following *as also saith the law. For Adam was formed first, then Eve, and Adam was not deceived, but the woman being deceived fell into transgression.* This shows how God enforced His law when giving His word to man; therefore, we are to enforce His word and law in the exact same way.

We continue to see God's unwavering firm decision to have the male be the public figure through the offspring that God gave to Abraham. God specifically chose to give Abraham a male child because it would be through this male child that God would establish His covenant with. As it says in Genesis 17:15-19 KJV:

"And God said unto Abraham, as for Sarai thy wife, thou shalt not call her name Sarai, but Sarah shall her name be. And I will bless her, and give thee a son also of her: yea, I will bless her, and she shall be a mother of nations; kings of people shall be of her. Then Abraham fell upon his face, and laughed, and said in his heart, shall a child be born unto him that is an hundred years old? And shall Sarah, that is

ninety years old, bear? And Abraham said unto God, O that Ishmael might live before thee! And God said, Sarah thy wife shall bear thee a son indeed; and thou shalt call his name Isaac: and I will establish my covenant with him for an everlasting covenant, and with his seed after him."

The intentionality from God in this set of verses is in the fact that God, who creates all life, determined to give Abraham a son, His specific selection of a male child to bless Abraham with in establishing His covenant. The importance of the statements made in this set of verses from God shows that the male is to lead not only with worship but with the entirety of His covenant, which covered multitudes of people.

However, this was not solely for the physical descendants of Abraham to see and acknowledge but for all nations to see, acknowledge, and understand that God has specifically chosen the male to establish His covenant with and lead the way in the giving and teaching of the laws of God, who would bless them and protect them if the people choose to obey His word. When Isaac is born to Abraham and Sarah and later comes of age, he marries Rebekah, and they have children, namely Esau and Jacob. While Rebekah is pregnant with Esau and Jacob, we continue to see God implementing the authority/subjection law with His intention to specifically use the male to establish two nations, as seen in Genesis 25:23 KJV:

"And the Lord said unto her, Two nations in thy womb, and two manner of people shall be separated from thy bowels; and the one people shall be stronger than the other people; and the elder shall serve the younger."

What we see and know God is doing in establishing these two different communities of people that are known worldwide is that He is following the pattern from the beginning, specifically selecting the male to lead nations of people. Particularly with Jacob, this nation represented God. Emphasis is again placed on the male as the sole public figure to represent God. Since God is following the pattern from the beginning in selecting the male, by which He chooses Jacob to lead a nation to represent Him, this additionally lets us know that the authority/subjection law covers more than just the order of worship when the congregation meets on the first day of the week. God's implementation of this law was inclusive of establishing a nation recognized globally. We further see this truth in the very definition of the name that God chose to give Jacob after a certain point, which is found in Genesis 32:25-28 KJV:

"Now when He saw that He did not prevail against him, He touched the socket of his hip; and the socket of Jacob's hip was out of joint as He wrestled with him. And He said, Let Me go, for the day breaks. But he said, I will not let You go unless You bless me! So He said to him, What is your name? He said, Jacob. And He said, Your name shall no longer be called Jacob, but Israel; for you have struggled with God and with men, and have prevailed."

God chose a male, and God chose to give Jacob a name that is defined as **he will rule as God,** which is the name **Israel.** This name is a statement given by God Himself to Jacob, which indicates how God rules. There are a few questions that we need to ask and allow the scriptures to answer. The first question that needs to be asked is: has God ever in scripture specifically sought out the woman for public rule, authority, or teaching in any capacity such as we see here with Jacob? Representing God amongst the nations in the public sphere?

Second, when God assigned this name to Jacob to make a nation out of his lineage, was the nation to rule amongst themselves, or was the nation to rule among the other nations in hopes of bringing those in darkness to light through the teachings of God?

Third, was God to be represented through the name given to Jacob and ultimately through the physical nation of Israel?

In answering the first question, we refer to God's specific decision to solely use men on the public platform from the beginning. With the lack of any women being used as public servants by God from the beginning, whether in worship or any area of the public arena to influence a multitude of men and women simultaneously in Godly living—such as what God does with the man—signifies how God views public authority and public teaching. The meaning of the name Israel being **he will rule as God** lets us know that the ruling that Israel would do would be equivalent to the ruling that God does, thus meaning that God would rule through Israel, by giving Israel His precepts in His Law; a body of people meant to be set apart from the error of the world to rule amongst the nations, to show the nations that His standard must be obeyed in order for God's acceptance. And notice the definition begins with "*he.*" The nation Israel being the lineage of Jacob, of whom he is the patriarch, head, and leader of this body of people. The one God has chosen to rule through.

This is a public platform on the global stage, and God chose a male for this purpose. With that said, does God rule publicly overall, or is His rule confined to Israel and the worship that was established within that nation by God? We know that it's the former and not the latter, as God rules over all. I call your attention to Ezekiel 20:8-9 KJV:

"But they rebelled against me, and would not hearken unto me: they did not every man cast away the abominations of their eyes, neither did they forsake the idols of Egypt: then I said, I will pour out my fury

upon them, to accomplish my anger against them in the midst of the land of Egypt. But I wrought for my name's sake, that it should not be polluted before the heathen, among whom they were, in whose sight I made myself known unto them, in bringing them forth out of the land of Egypt."

With particular emphasis on the nations, notice what God said here in verse 9: His name should not be polluted among the nations, as the nations saw when God made Himself known to Israel. What this lets us know is that who God is and the marvelous works He did for Israel were to be a positive influence on all nations, and the nations were to recognize the intrinsic nature and indispensable qualities of God and conclude that there is no other like Him. Thus, confirming that Israel, of whom God ruled through and of whom God specifically chose a male named Jacob to lead this nation, which took on his name, was to rule publicly amongst all nations. Additionally, in answering our second question at hand, was the nation to rule amongst themselves, or was the nation to rule among the other nations in hopes of bringing those in darkness to light through the teachings of God? Scripture in the New Testament tells us this much as well when the apostle Paul writes his letter to the Romans in Romans 2:17-19 KJV:

"Behold, thou art called a Jew, and restest in the law, and makest thy boast of God And knowest his will, and approvest the things that are more excellent, being instructed out of the law; And art confident that thou thyself art a guide of the blind, a light of them which are in darkness."

The nation of Israel was to publicly be the example to the world, showing the world, who God is by obedience to His law, and what was always inclusive of God's law from the beginning is what the apostle Paul discusses in 1 Corinthians 14:34 and 1 Timothy 2:11-15. We not only see this law enforced by God Himself by His choosing of the male for public communication in the patriarchal age, but also in the Law of Moses. We see the public figure is the patriarch; Abraham, who is heir of the world, being the example to Jew and Gentile alike for how one is justified by God, and Jacob, the grandson of Abraham, whom God specifically chose in giving him the name that reflects God ruling through his lineage to rule amongst the nations.

This is a fact and example for the Lord's church as well. The church is now the Israel of God, which is spiritual Israel, for all who have obeyed the gospel of Jesus Christ being justified the same way Abraham was, making all who obey the gospel the children of Abraham; Jew and Gentile alike. This was Paul's primary point in writing his letter to the Galatians as he concludes in Galatians 6:15-16 KJV:

"For in Christ Jesus neither circumcision availeth anything, nor uncircumcision, but a new creature. And as many as walk according to this rule, peace be on them, and mercy, and upon the Israel of God."

In answering our third question, was God to be represented through the name given to Jacob and ultimately through the physical nation of Israel? I call your attention to two statements: a statement made by Gideon in Judges 8:22-23 KJV and a statement that God made about Israel regarding their rejection of Him in 1 Samuel 8:6-7 KJV.

Judges 8:22-23 KJV:

"Then the men of Israel said unto Gideon, Rule thou over us, both thou, and thy son, and thy son's son also: for thou hast delivered us from the hand of Midian. And Gideon said unto them, I will not rule over you, neither shall my son rule over you: the Lord shall rule over you."

And 1 Samuel 8:6-7 KJV:

"But the thing displeased Samuel, when they said, Give us a king to judge us. And Samuel prayed unto the Lord and the Lord said unto Samuel, Hearken unto the voice of the people in all that they say unto thee: for they have not rejected thee, but they have rejected me, that I should not reign over them."

To put to rest any objection regarding the public rule the fleshly nation of Israel had amongst the nations, it should be noted that physical Israel served as a shadow of spiritual Israel, of which Christ now reigns as King of kings. Does Christ reign in His church among the entirety of humanity, or is His reign limited to His church? Does the church reign among the kingdoms of the world, or does the church reign amongst themselves? The point to understand in why this is important is because of the pattern established by God when enforcing His word.

Another factual point to consider is that with the church now known as the Israel of God, this lets us know that this is how God rules: through Jesus Christ instead of the Law of Moses. Yet the same standard is implemented with the Lord in the gospel as it was under the Patriarchal and Mosaic ages, with the statement *"as also saith the law"* (authority/subjection law) under consideration in 1 Corinthians 14:34 and 1 Timothy 2:8-15. Israel, now the church, is how God rules. And as we have seen, God intentionally assigned that name to a male, thus showing by patterned example, inclusive of the lack of God's intentional use of the female in the public arena, the Godly enforcement of what *"as also saith the law"* means. The male, in accordance with His law, is the sole authority by scriptural implementation with God's approval to speak on His behalf in the public arena to male and female simultaneously; a body of people of whom God rules through.

An imperative point of understanding that we must also acknowledge is the order in which God communicates His will to humanity in the public arena, meaning Jew and Gentile simultaneously. Not only do we see God's deliberate choice of the male, but He furthermore concludes this is the divine order *(the law)* that He follows when we look at 1 Corinthians 11:3 KJV:

"But I would have you know, that the head of every man is Christ; and the head of the woman is the man; and the head of Christ is God."

One must ask: Is Christ only the head of every man in His church, or is He the head of every man? Does Christ's word only apply to His church, or does it apply to all of humanity? Scripture concludes He is the head of all humanity and His word applies to all of humanity, *for there is none other name under heaven given among men, whereby we must be saved* (Acts 4:12 KJV). God the Father communicates through Christ for salvation for the entire world; this is enforced publicly. What scripture also shows us is that every time God has communicated His will for humanity in the public arena, He has always used the male because God is keeping in accordance with His law, which is the divine order being discussed here. Evidence is also seen in the male children of Jacob (Israel). Jacob had a total of 13 children: 1 daughter and 12 sons.

Genesis 34:1 KJV:
"And Dinah the daughter of Leah, which she bare unto Jacob, went out to see the daughters of the land."

And Genesis 35:22 KJV:
"And it came to pass, when Israel dwelt in that land, that Reuben went and lay with Bilhah his father's concubine: and Israel heard it. Now the sons of Jacob were twelve."

Out of his 13 children, the tribes of Israel were named after the 12 male children and the male children of those 12 children, namely here Ephraim and Manasseh, the children of Joseph. Genesis 48:14-19 KJV:

"And Israel stretched out his right hand, and laid it upon Ephraim's head, who was the younger, and his left hand upon Manasseh's head, guiding his hands wittingly; for Manasseh was the firstborn. And he blessed Joseph, and said, God, before whom my fathers Abraham and Isaac did walk, the God which fed me all my life long unto this day, the Angel which redeemed me from all evil, bless the lads; and let my name be named on them, and the name of my fathers Abraham and Isaac; and let them grow into a multitude in the midst of the earth. And when Joseph saw that his father laid his right hand upon the head of Ephraim, it displeased him: and he held up his father's hand, to remove it from Ephraim's head unto Manasseh's head. And Joseph said unto his father, Not so, my father: for this is the firstborn; put thy right hand upon his head. And his father refused, and said, I know it, my son, I know it: he also shall become a people, and he also shall be great: but truly his younger brother shall be greater than he, and his seed shall become a multitude of nations."

The tribes of the children of Jacob were comprised of all fleshly children of Israel, and they were amenable to all aspects of societal and legal life under the law of Moses. Why was there not a tribe named after Dinah, Jacob's only daughter? In looking at the Hebrew words for tribe, which are Matteh and Mattah, they are defined as a branch (as extending), a rod for chastising, and ruling (a scepter). Based on the definition of tribe, this means that one who the tribe is named after is considered the authority and ruling figure for the said division of people. The fact that the tribes comprised all of societal life and the absence of a tribe after Dinah further demonstrates the lack of public authority that females had in societal life, which is in conjunction with the intentional enforcement of the law the apostle Paul discusses in 1 Timothy 2:12 and shows to what extent this authority covers within the word of God. Through God's choosing, we do not see the female in any authoritative role in society, with the implementation of God's word, inclusive of tribal representation.

Because it is God who is enforcing these standards as He enacts His law, the conclusion follows that the standards are not only a part of the law of Moses, but because this standard was implemented before the law of Moses, as we have seen throughout the book of Genesis, this standard has always been law from the beginning. As the Israeli people multiplied in Egypt and were under bondage for 400 years, all of which God told Abraham would take place in Genesis 15:13 KJV:

"And he said unto Abram, Know of a surety that thy seed shall be a stranger in a land that is not theirs, and shall serve them; and they shall afflict them four hundred years."

God had a time prepared to deliver the children of Israel out of bondage, and He did so by His servant Moses and Aaron, as the following sets of scripture detail: Exodus 3:9-10 KJV:

"Now therefore, behold, the cry of the children of Israel is come unto me: and I have also seen the oppression wherewith the Egyptians oppress them. Come now therefore, and I will send thee unto Pharaoh, that thou mayest bring forth my people the children of Israel out of Egypt."

And Exodus 4:14 KJV:

"And the anger of the Lord was kindled against Moses, and he said, Is not Aaron the Levite thy brother? I know that he can speak well. And also, behold, he cometh forth to meet thee: and when he seeth thee, he will be glad in his heart."

As we see God using Moses and Aaron to bring Israel out with great substance, which was the plan revealed to Abraham by God. What necessary inference concludes here is that the selecting of a male to lead Israel out of Egypt was also a part of God's plan. To further drive this point home, I call your attention to Psalm 105:23-26 KJV:

"Israel also came into Egypt; and Jacob sojourned in the land of Ham. And he increased his people greatly; and made them stronger than their enemies. He turned their heart to hate his people, to deal subtilly with his servants. He sent Moses his servant; and Aaron whom he had chosen."

As we examine God's plan and implementation of it with the physical nation of Israel and compare it to the statement *"as also saith the law"* with its definition explained in 1 Corinthians 14:34 and 1 Timothy 2:8-15, three observations can be seen here. First, when God chose to publicly reveal Himself to this pagan nation by the speaking of His word, it was through Moses. The authority is established and set by God for Moses and Aaron to speak to a nation and for God to work miracles by Moses's hand. Critical to our understanding of the authority at hand in publicly speaking on behalf of God to man and woman simultaneously is the fact that it is God who has given the word, and He has repeatedly shown a pattern of using a specific type of earthen vessel to convey His message publicly. The enforcement of the earthen vessel that God chooses to use to convey His word shows the approval of authority that vessel has from God. With the repeated pattern of the specific earthen vessel God chooses to use on the public platform being male in every scriptural instance, the necessary inference of 1 Timothy 2:8-15 and *"as also saith the law"* in 1 Corinthians 14:34 confirms the limitations on publicly usurping authority and teaching the male by the woman extend outside of the worship assembly and cover the entire public arena; God's enforcement shows the extent of the law.

Secondly, throughout the entirety of the situation between Moses and Pharaoh, praying was involved by request of Pharaoh to Moses and on Moses' behalf as well for Pharaoh. Scripture tells us this in Exodus 8:28-29 KJV:

"And Pharaoh said, I will let you go, that ye may sacrifice to the Lord your God in the wilderness; only ye shall not go very far away: intreat for me. And Moses said, Behold, I go out from thee, and I will intreat the Lord that the swarms of flies may depart from Pharaoh, from his servants, and from his people, to morrow: but let not Pharaoh deal deceitfully any more in not letting the people go to sacrifice to the Lord."

And Exodus 10:16-18 KJV:

"Then Pharaoh called for Moses and Aaron in haste; and he said, I have sinned against the Lord your God, and against you. Now therefore forgive, I pray thee, my sin only this once, and intreat the Lord your God, that he may take away from me this death only. And he went out from Pharaoh, and intreated the Lord."

When God sent Moses and Aaron to Pharaoh, working miraculously through them to release Israel from Egypt, He performed the ten plagues, which were known and witnessed in every corner of Egyptian society, thus making the plagues a public event. What is interesting to note is, as we've read in Psalm 105:26, God chose Moses and Aaron in accordance with His plan. In this situation, Moses prayed for Pharaoh on two separate occasions after a public display from God through Moses, and this was in accordance with the standard in God's plan of choosing the male to do so; this is equal to the standard stated in 1 Timothy 2:8 of the male praying in every place. There is no worship assembly nor gathering to praise God on these occasions, yet we see a chosen standard applied by God that matches the standard discussed by the apostle Paul under the gospel of Christ in 1 Corinthians 14:34 and 1 Timothy 2:8-15. Because God applied this standard before the worship assembly of the New Testament and outside of worship to Him in the Old Testament, and evidence shows this standard is still applied in the gospel of Christ by its implementation, as confirmed by the statement "***as also saith the law***" in 1 Corinthians 14:33, then what authority do we have to change a standard that God has applied throughout the entirety of man's history?

Third, all of this took place before the system of worship was established for the Israeli nation. It is often thought that the law Paul speaks of is an extension of how the worship system for Israel was applied under the law of Moses, meaning that because it was the men leading worship under the law of Moses, therefore Paul's statements just reiterate this same concept in the gospel. However, the connotation that 1 Corinthians 14:34 and 1 Timothy 2:8-15 only applies to worship is a great disservice to the statement "as also saith the law," because of how it is defined and how God enacts this law by whom He chose to carry out public teaching on His behalf. At the time of Moses's praying for Pharaoh, God had not yet given Moses the law, as Pharaoh had not yet let Israel out of Egypt, yet we see the method of operation that God planned to use, has used, and always used was a specific choice of the male for every public and societal occasion on His behalf.

9

Background To The Levitical Priesthood

After the final plague sent by God towards Pharaoh and the Egyptians, Pharaoh let Israel go from Egypt. Yet Pharaoh had a change of heart and decided to take the Egyptian army and come after Israel because of his desire to have the Israelites serve him. The Israelites doubted God and Moses as they saw the Egyptian army coming to seize them, but the Lord was working through His servant Moses, who said to Israel in Exodus 14:13 KJV:

"Fear ye not, stand still and see the salvation of the Lord."

The Lord fought for Israel and saved them, as Exodus 14:31 KJV says:
"And Israel saw that great work which the Lord did upon the Egyptians: and the people feared the Lord, and believed the Lord, and his servant Moses."

Moving forward from this point, God had in mind that the whole nation of Israel was to be a kingdom of priests and a holy nation, as Exodus 19:3-7 KJV tells us:

"And Moses went up unto God, and the Lord called unto him out of

the mountain, saying, Thus shalt thou say to the house of Jacob, and tell the children of Israel. Ye have seen what I did unto the Egyptians, and how I bare you on eagles' wings, and brought you unto myself. Now therefore, if ye will obey my voice indeed, and keep my covenant, then ye shall be a peculiar treasure unto me above all people: for all the earth is mine And ye shall be unto me a kingdom of priests, and an holy nation. These are the words which thou shalt speak unto the children of Israel. And Moses came and called for the elders of the people, and laid before their faces all these words which the Lord commanded him."

Of particular emphasis in this set of verses, I would like to draw your attention to three statements God made in verses 6-7: *"***you shall be unto me a kingdom of priests, and an holy nation***"* and *"***Moses came and called for the elders of the people.***"* Kingdom of priests, an holy nation, called for the elders of the people.

When God led Israel out of Egypt under the tutelage of Moses, His intention was for the whole nation of Israel to be a kingdom of priests. This includes both male and female, as both genders made up the entire nation. At first, all within Israel were to be known as set apart, offering sacrifices to God; however, look at whom Moses called for after God spoke with him concerning these things in Exodus 19:6: *"**the elders."*** This is a significant point because, though it was God's initial intention for all of Israel to be known as a kingdom of priests, the calling for the elders (**the men**) of Israel lets us know at least two things.

First, this indicates the normal function of the men as leaders among the people as a whole, inclusive of all social standards. We know this to be factual because, at this point, the law for worship had still not been fully given to Israel. Though God intended for all of Israel to be a kingdom of priests, ultimately only the Levites made up the priesthood because they committed themselves to follow God when the rest of Israel began to sin. As evidence shows in Exodus 32:25-29 KJV:

"And when Moses saw that the people were naked; (for Aaron had made them naked unto their shame among their enemies:) Then Moses stood in the gate of the camp, and said, who is on the Lord's side? let him come unto me. And all the sons of Levi gathered themselves together unto him. And he said unto them, thus saith the Lord God of Israel, put every man his sword by his side, and go in and out from gate to gate throughout the camp, and slay every man his brother, and every man his companion, and every man his neighbour. And the children of Levi did according to the word of Moses: and there fell of the people that day about three thousand men. For Moses had said, consecrate yourselves today to the Lord, even every man upon his son, and upon his brother; that he may bestow upon you a blessing this day."

With the case being the normal function of men leading in society, we see the practice and standard was for the prophet of God to speak to the men publicly, who were to communicate God's law to their families regarding how they were to live before God. Additionally, when we look closer at verses 6 and 7, we see an order that God confirms elsewhere in Scripture; when God tells Moses these are the words which thou shalt speak to the children of Israel, Moses immediately came and **called for the elders of the people, and laid before their faces all these words which the Lord commanded him.** This is equivalent to speaking to all the children of Israel because the Scripture tells us that Moses did what the Lord commanded. This order is also confirmed in a verse that we have previously discussed, found in 1 Corinthians 11:3 KJV:

"The head of every man is Christ, the head of every woman is man, and the head of Christ is God."

Second, there is another scripture within the gospel of Christ that confirms the facts of the Old Testament history that we are examining, which is Hebrews 1:1 KJV:

"God, who at sundry times and in divers manners spake in time past unto the fathers by the prophets."

When looking closely at what is stated and confirmed in this verse, it is a fact that we see a method of operation or standard being applied. This means that when God wanted to reveal His word to man during the time before Christ in the Old Testament, He would repeatedly seek the male prophets to speak on His behalf to the fathers; this is precisely what God does with the example of Moses, who is a prophet and speaks to the elders of Israel. By this, we see an intentional standard established by the highest authority, which is God, showing He specifically sought the male to convey His message. We know that this standard included all public platforms because Hebrews 1:1 is contrasted with Jesus in Hebrews 1:2 KJV:

"Hath in these last days spoken unto us by His Son whom He hath appointed heir of all things by whom also He made the worlds."

God transcends time in speaking to all of mankind throughout the world through His Son Jesus by the written gospel of Christ, the New Testament scriptures. In comparison to the public speaking of Jesus, this confirms that the revelations spoken in portions by the prophets from God were also delivered in public fashion prior to Christ; the only difference being that full revelation is found in Christ, as opposed to the limited revelation in the prophets. This standard that God specifically sought is shown to be the law that Paul discusses in our core scriptures of 1 Corinthians 14:34 and 1 Timothy 2:8-15, as well as what we see in Exodus 19:6-7. From this, we understand that God commanded His prophet Moses to speak to the elders because this was God's law: that the male is the one with the authority from God to publicly speak His will, as the elders in Exodus 19:6-7 had to convey the words of Moses from God to the masses within each tribe of Israel. We know this to be true because of what is stated in Exodus 19:8 KJV:

"And all the people answered together, and said, all that the Lord hath spoken we will do. And Moses returned the words of the people unto the Lord."

As we look further into the statements made regarding the functioning of the priesthood and how it ultimately was given to the Levitical tribe, let us examine a couple of commandments made by God and spoken through Moses that were given in Exodus chapters 12 and 13. First, I call your attention to Exodus 12:21-27 KJV:

"Then Moses called for all the elders of Israel, and said unto them, Draw out and take you a lamb according to your families, and kill the Passover. And ye shall take a bunch of hyssop, and dip it in the blood that is in the bason, and strike the lintel and the two side posts with the blood that is in the bason; and none of you shall go out at the door of his house until the morning. For the Lord will pass through to smite the Egyptians; and when he seeth the blood upon the lintel, and on the two side posts, the Lord will pass over the door, and will not suffer the destroyer to come in unto your houses to smite you. And ye shall observe this thing for an ordinance to thee and to thy sons forever. And it shall come to pass, when ye be come to the land which the Lord will give you, according as he hath promised, that ye shall keep this service. And it shall come to pass, when your children shall say unto you, what mean ye by this service? That ye shall say, it is the sacrifice of the Lord's Passover, who passed over the houses of the children of Israel in Egypt, when he smote the Egyptians, and delivered our houses. And the people bowed the head and worshipped."

As Moses was preparing Israel for the Passover, which would lead to Pharaoh letting Israel go, there are three things worthy of mention in this set of verses. First, as we've previously mentioned, Moses was speaking to the elders; however, not only was he speaking to the elders, but he gave them a direct command as to what exactly they were to do. The command for the elders to take a lamb, kill the Passover, and take hyssop, dip it into the blood, and strike the lintel and two side posts are public acts that had to be done so the destroyer would not come into their houses. What is seen here is God commanding the men through Moses to lead publicly in doing this service. With the Israeli people composed of both males and females, God chose the males to conduct these public acts at His command, confirming by scriptural example that the male has been tasked with the function of being the sole leader in public on behalf of God.

Second, this was a public service of sacrifice to the Lord. In this set of verses, we have the first mention of Passover for the people of Israel. Looking at Exodus 12:24-27, the Passover was to be included in the worship of Israel when they came into the land that the Lord gave them. The individuals who were to function in the role of conducting the Passover are referred to by Moses in Exodus 12:21 as "the elders." This sacrifice to the Lord was to be kept in worship to the Lord, and it was assigned to the men to conduct. But why did God specifically assign this task to the men? It is because God based this on a preexisting standard that was already in place before He established the worship system for the Israelite people, and that preexisting standard is seen throughout the book of Genesis and in Moses calling for the elders (men). Moses followed God's order by addressing the elders because God has exclusively assigned the male the role of publicly leading. Since worship is a public sacrificing of what God has commanded, we see nothing new established with the men leading in worship, just a continuation of what was already in place. This further confirms what the apostle Paul discussed in 1 Corinthians 14:34, "as also saith the law," and 1 Timothy 2:8-15.

Third, the elders were tasked with the responsibility of teaching the children of Israel the meaning of the Passover and the commandment to keep it. As we've been discussing, what we see from God in how He conveys His commandments and His word to man is patterned behavior through God's implementation of His word. He commanded Moses from the beginning to gather the elders together and speak to them His word. This is what we see in Exodus 3:16 KJV:

"Go, and gather the elders of Israel together, and say unto them, The Lord God of your fathers, the God of Abraham, of Isaac, and of Jacob, appeared unto me, saying, I have surely visited you, and seen that which is done to you in Egypt."

As we also look further in Exodus 3:18, it was not only commanded for Moses and Aaron to go to Pharaoh, but also the elders were to go with them, as it reads:

"And they shall hearken to thy voice: and thou shalt come, thou and the elders of Israel, unto the king of Egypt, and ye shall say unto him, The Lord God of the Hebrews hath met with us: and now let us go, we beseech thee, three days' journey into the wilderness, that we may sacrifice to the Lord our God."

By God specifically telling His prophet Moses to gather the elders and calling for the elders to be present with Moses and Aaron, it automatically brings attention to the status of the men in society; God is acknowledging that the men were responsible for being the public leaders. Additionally, a fact that needs to be mentioned is that when God gives His law, it is His will for man; which, by legal terms, He is known as the Testator. Whom God appoints to follow the instructions of His will is known as the Executor. With particular emphasis on His law that Paul has addressed in 1 Corinthians 14:34 and 2 Timothy 2:8-15, what we have been calling the authority/subjection law—because God has chosen the men in every public platform to lead on His behalf throughout the scriptures, with focus being given here on the elders—shows that God has appointed the male as Executor of His law (will) for who is to publicly teach God's word. The example given in Exodus 3:16-18 confirms why the elders were also tasked with the responsibility to teach in Exodus 12:27.

Two additional verses that confirm the elders were tasked with the responsibility of teaching are evident in Exodus 24:12 KJV:
"And the Lord said unto Moses, Come up to me into the mount, and be there: and I will give thee tables of stone, and a law, and commandments which I have written; that thou mayest teach them."

Why this verse holds significance to our discussion is that with Moses being the prophet of God, he relayed what God taught him to the elders, as we've mentioned earlier in this section with Exodus 19:6-8 and Hebrews 1:1-2. We further see Moses with the elders teaching the commandments of God in Deuteronomy 27:1 KJV:
"And Moses with the elders of Israel commanded the people, saying, keep all the commandments which I command you this day."

Additionally, as we've stated at the onset of this section, in like manner with Exodus 12, looking at Exodus 13:11-15, we now understand why God chose the firstborn male of animal and man, as it reads:
"And it shall be when the Lord shall bring thee into the land of the Canaanites, as He sware unto thee and to thy fathers, and shall give it thee that thou shalt set apart unto the Lord all that openeth the matrix,

and every firstling that cometh of a beast which thou hast; the males shall be the Lord and every firstling of an ass thou shalt redeem with a lamb; and if thou wilt not redeem it, then thou shalt break his neck: and all the firstborn of man among thy children shalt thou redeem. And it shall be when thy son asketh thee in time to come, saying, what is this? that thou shalt say unto him, by strength of hand the Lord brought us out from Egypt, from the house of bondage. And it came to pass, when Pharaoh would hardly let us go, that the Lord slew all the firstborn in the land of Egypt, both the firstborn of man, and the firstborn of beast: therefore I sacrifice to the Lord all that openeth the matrix, being males; but all the firstborn of my children I redeem."

Though initially it was God's intention to have the entire nation of Israel be priests, it ultimately was given only to the tribe of Levi (Levites) because of their commitment to follow God when the rest of Israel fell into sin, as we've seen in Exodus chapter 32. As the priesthood was given to the Levites, we see the laws and order that God put in place for the Levitical priesthood in Leviticus chapters 1-10, which covered the laws for sin offerings, peace offerings, the priest and his offering, the consecration of Aaron and his sons, God's acceptance of Aaron's offering, and the death of Nadab and Abihu. As God is implementing His law by the male Levites for the priesthood, we see throughout these chapters that it is the men commanded to the functioning role of leading the worship; God has commanded this because worship is a public setting (Lev. 1:3, 12:7). Further underlining the fact of the law, God has reserved the role of the male for public teaching on His behalf. His pattern of implementing and selecting shows His approval is solely for the male.

This point is further extended with the commands that God gave Moses in Numbers Chapters 3-4, where God specifically commanded Moses to count the males one month old and up under the tribe of Levi, after the house of their fathers, by their families, e.g., Numbers 3:15 KJV:

"Number the children of Levi after the house of their fathers, by their families: every male from a month old and upward shalt thou number them."

Out of all tribes among the children of Levi, the emphasis is placed on the male to the very early age of one month old. The priority of the fathers and the males, as designated by God of all under Levi, signifies not only their authority in worship but also in society. The males were to be taught to lead publicly according to the word of God and by the example of how God implanted His standard.

As God is establishing the laws of Israel, which is how Israel was to function, we are reminded of the meaning of the name of Israel, *"He will rule as God."* God shows who has the authority to lead publicly through His selection of the male. A further example is seen in three additional sets of verses. The first is Numbers 1:2-4 KJV:

"Take ye the sum of all the congregation of the children of Israel, after their families, by the house of their fathers, with the number of their names, every male by their polls; From twenty years old and upward, all that are able to go forth to war in Israel: thou and Aaron shall number them by their armies. And with you there shall be a man of every tribe; every one head of the house of his fathers."

The second is Deuteronomy 1:11-15 KJV:

"(The Lord God of your fathers make you a thousand times so many more as ye are, and bless you, as he hath promised you!). How can I myself alone bear your cumbrance, and your burden, and your strife take you wise men, and understanding, and known among your tribes, and I will make them rulers over you and ye answered me, and said,

the thing which thou hast spoken is good for us to do so I took the chief of your tribes, wise men, and known, and made them heads over you, captains over thousands, and captains over hundreds, and captains over fifties, and captains over tens, and officers among your tribes."

And third is Deuteronomy 16:18-20 KJV:

"Judges and officers shalt thou make thee in all thy gates, which the Lord thy God giveth thee, throughout thy tribes: and they shall judge the people with just judgment. Thou shalt not wrest judgment; thou shalt not respect persons, neither take a gift: for a gift doth blind the eyes of the wise, and pervert the words of the righteous. That which is altogether just shalt thou follow, that thou mayest live, and inherit the land which the Lord thy God giveth thee."

The God-commanding standard for society in Israel was for the males to be counted as they were to be the public figures among the people in military battle, settling disputes, and setting the order of societal life. We see this same standard transcend time under Israeli history as we study the Law of Moses throughout the pages of Old Testament scripture. This same standard is also seen prior to Moses in the book of Genesis. By God setting the standard with the command He gave through His choosing of the male, it further confirms the authority/subjection law Paul discusses under the gospel of Christ is the standard God implemented in the Old Testament, going beyond the boundaries of worship and encompassing all public platforms.

Additionally, one should not conclude that God chose the men because there was a lack of women or that the women were outnumbered by the men. The reason we cannot draw such a conclusion is that Luke 1:5 KJV tells us that Aaron (who was high priest) had a lineage of daughters, and one of them was named Elizabeth, as it says:

> *"There was, in the days of Herod, the king of Judaea, a certain priest named Zacharias, of the course of Abia; and his wife was of the daughters of Aaron, and her name was Elisabeth."*

As we notice Elizabeth and her husband Zacharias in Luke chapter 1, we see that these individuals were walking in all the commandments of God. Luke 1:6 KJV states:

> *"And they were both righteous before God, walking in all the commandments and ordinances of the Lord blameless."*

Approximately 1,500 years passed from when God gave Israel the law of Moses to when Elizabeth and Zacharias conceived John the Baptist, who was born under this same law of Moses. This husband-and-wife duo is found to be blameless before God as they walked in all the commandments and ordinances of the Lord, confirming that the commandments given by God at the inception of the law of Moses stood throughout the history of the fleshly nation of Israel. This means that even though Aaron had a lineage of daughters, God, by commandment, chose the men to function in every aspect of Israel's public domain. Elizabeth, the daughter of Aaron who was righteous in keeping with all of God's commandments, acknowledged the functions that were given to male and female, just as her husband Zacharias did, who was a priest in Israel.

Conclusion

In conclusion; with the question asked in the title of this book, Can Women Use Public Platforms to Teach Men the Gospel of Christ? Based on the God-given and implemented standard discussed here, as detailed in the scriptures, the answer is no. As it goes with today's culture; times may have changed from the 1st century, but the God-given standard remains the same. Any public platform used in today's day, and age has this Divine law bound to it. I humbly implore those who oppose the principles laid out here with the scriptures outlined to please scripturally show where the arguments made here in this discussion are false. If it cannot scripturally be proven false then the position taken in opposition to the scriptural standard laid out here is false, and to uphold a scripturally false position is to be in opposition to God.

Appendix

The Hebrew Word Mashal Used For Public Authority

Highlighted in bold

Genesis 1:18

"And to **rule** over the day and over the night, and to divide the light from the darkness: and God saw that it was good."

Genesis 3:16

"Unto the woman he said, I will greatly multiply thy sorrow and thy conception; in sorrow thou shalt bring forth children; and thy desire shall be to thy husband, and he shall **rule** over thee."

Genesis 4:7

"If thou doest well, shalt thou not be accepted? and if thou doest not well, sin lieth at the door. And unto thee shall be his desire, and thou shalt **rule** over him."

Genesis 24:2

"And Abraham said unto his eldest servant of his house, that **ruled** over all that he had, Put, I pray thee, thy hand under my thigh."

Genesis 37:8

"And his brethren said to him, Shalt thou indeed reign over us? or shalt thou indeed have **dominion** over us? And they hated him yet the more for his dreams, and for his words."

Genesis 45:8

"So now it was not you that sent me hither, but God: and he hath made me a father to Pharaoh, and lord of all his house, and a **ruler** throughout all the land of Egypt."

Genesis 45:26

"And told him, saying, Joseph is yet alive, and he is **governor** over all the land of Egypt. And Jacob's heart fainted, for he believed them not."

Exodus 21:8

"If she please not her master, who hath betrothed her to himself, then shall he let her be redeemed: to sell her unto a strange nation he shall have no **power**, seeing he hath dealt deceitfully with her."

Deuteronomy 15:6

"For the Lord thy God blesseth thee, as he promised thee: and thou shalt lend unto many nations, but thou shalt not borrow; and thou shalt **reign** over many nations, but they shall not **reign** over thee."

Joshua 12:5

"And **reigned** in mount Hermon, and in Salcah, and in all Bashan, unto the border of the Geshurites and the Maachathites, and half Gilead, the border of Sihon king of Heshbon."

Judges 8:22

"Then the men of Israel said unto Gideon, **Rule** thou over us, both thou, and thy son, and thy son's son also: for thou hast delivered us from the hand of Midian."

Judges 8:23

"And Gideon said unto them, I will not **rule** over you, neither shall my son **rule** over you: the Lord shall **rule** over you."

Judges 9:2

"Speak, I pray you, in the ears of all the men of Shechem, Whether is better for you, either that all the sons of Jerubbaal, which are threescore and ten persons, **reign** over you, or that one **reign** over you? remember also that I am your bone and your flesh."

Judges 14:4

"But his father and his mother knew not that it was of the Lord, that he sought an occasion against the Philistines: for at that time the Philistines had **dominion** over Israel."

Judges 15:11

"Then three thousand men of Judah went to the top of the rock Etam, and said to Samson, Knowest thou not that the Philistines are **rulers** over us? what is this that thou hast done unto us? And he said unto them, as they did unto me, so have I done unto them."

2 Samuel 23:3

"The God of Israel said, the Rock of Israel spake to me, He that **ruleth** over men must be just, ruling in the fear of God."

1 Kings 4:21

"And Solomon **reigned** over all kingdoms from the river unto the land of the Philistines, and unto the border of Egypt: they brought presents, and served Solomon all the days of his life."

1 Chronicles 29:12

"Both riches and honour come of thee, and thou **reignest** over all; and in thine hand is power and might; and in thine hand it is to make great, and to give strength unto all."

2 Chronicles 7:18

"Then will I stablish the throne of thy kingdom, according as I have covenanted with David thy father, saying, there shall not fail thee a man to be **ruler** in Israel."

2 Chronicles 9:26

"And he **reigned** over all the kings from the river even unto the land of the Philistines, and to the border of Egypt."

2 Chronicles 20:6

"And said, O Lord God of our fathers, art not thou God in heaven? and **rulest** not thou over all the kingdoms of the heathen? and in thine hand is there not power and might, so that none is able to withstand thee?"

2 Chronicles 23:20

"And he took the captains of hundreds, and the nobles, and the **governors** of the people, and all the people of the land, and brought down the king from the house of the Lord: and they came through the high gate into the king's house, and set the king upon the throne of the kingdom."

Nehemiah 9:37

"And it yieldeth much increase unto the kings whom thou hast set over us because of our sins: also they have **dominion** over our bodies, and over our cattle, at their pleasure, and we are in great distress."

Job 25:2

"**Dominion** and fear are with him, he maketh peace in his high places."

Psalm 8:6

"Thou madest him to have **dominion** over the works of thy hands; thou hast put all things under his feet"

Psalm 19:13

"Keep back thy servant also from presumptuous sins; let them not have **dominion** over me: then shall I be upright, and I shall be innocent from the great transgression."

Psalm 22:28

"For the kingdom is the Lord's: and he is the **governor** among the nations."

Psalm 59:13

"Consume them in wrath, consume them, that they may not be: and let them know that God **ruleth** in Jacob unto the ends of the earth. Selah."

Psalm 66:7

"He **ruleth** by his power for ever; his eyes behold the nations: let not the rebellious exalt themselves. Selah."

Psalm 89:9

"Thou **rulest** the raging of the sea: when the waves thereof arise, thou stillest them."

Psalm 103:19

"The Lord hath prepared his throne in the heavens; and his kingdom **ruleth** over all."

Psalm 105:20

"The king sent and loosed him; even the **ruler** of the people, and let him go free."

Psalm 105:21
"He made him lord of his house, and **ruler** of all his substance."

Psalm 106:41
"And he gave them into the hand of the heathen; and they that hated them **ruled** over them."

Proverbs 6:7
"Which having no guide, overseer, or **ruler**."

Proverbs 12:24
"The hand of the diligent shall bear **rule**: but the slothful shall be under tribute."

Proverbs 16:32
"He that is slow to anger is better than the mighty; and he that **ruleth** his spirit than he that taketh a city."

Proverbs 17:2
"A wise servant shall have **rule** over a son that causeth shame, and shall have part of the inheritance among the brethren."

Proverbs 19:10

"Delight is not seemly for a fool; much less for a servant to have **rule** over princes"

Proverbs 22:7

"The rich **ruleth** over the poor, and the borrower is servant to the lender."

Proverbs 23:1

"When thou sittest to eat with a **ruler**, consider diligently what is before thee"

Proverbs 28:15

"As a roaring lion, and a ranging bear; so is a wicked **ruler** over the poor people."

Proverbs 29:2

"When the righteous are in authority, the people rejoice: but when the wicked beareth **rule**, the people mourn."

Proverbs 29:26

"Many seek the **ruler's** favour; but every man's judgment cometh from the Lord."

Ecclesiastes 9:17

"The words of wise men are heard in quiet more than the cry of him that

ruleth *among fools."*

Ecclesiastes 10:4
*"If the spirit of the **ruler** rise up against thee, leave not thy place; for yielding pacifieth great offences."*

Isaiah 3:4
*"And I will give children to be their princes, and babes shall **rule** over them."*

Isaiah 3:12
*"As for my people, children are their oppressors, and women **rule** over them. O my people, they which lead thee cause thee to err, and destroy the way of thy paths."*

Isaiah 14:5
*"The Lord hath broken the staff of the wicked, and the sceptre of the **rulers**."*

Isaiah 16:1
*"Send ye the lamb to the **ruler** of the land from Sela to the wilderness, unto the mount of the daughter of Zion."*

Isaiah 19:4
*"And the Egyptians will I give over into the hand of a cruel lord; and a fierce king shall **rule** over them, saith the Lord, the Lord of hosts."*

Isaiah 28:14

"Wherefore hear the word of the Lord, ye scornful men, that **rule** this people which is in Jerusalem."

Isaiah 40:10

"Behold, the Lord God will come with strong hand, and his arm shall **rule** for him: behold, his reward is with him, and his work before him."

Isaiah 49:7

"Thus saith the Lord, the Redeemer of Israel, and his Holy One, to him whom man despiseth, to him whom the nation abhorreth, to a servant of **rulers**, Kings shall see and arise, princes also shall worship, because of the Lord that is faithful, and the Holy One of Israel, and he shall choose thee."

Isaiah 52:5

"Now therefore, what have I here, saith the Lord, that my people is taken away for nought? they that **rule** over them make them to howl, saith the Lord; and my name continually every day is blasphemed."

Isaiah 63:19

"We are thine: thou never barest **rule** over them; they were not called by thy name."

Jeremiah 22:30

"Thus saith the Lord, write ye this man childless, a man that shall not prosper in his days: for no man of his seed shall prosper, sitting upon the *throne of David, and **ruling** any more in Judah."*

Jeremiah 30:21

"And their nobles shall be of themselves, and their **governor** shall proceed from the midst of them; and I will cause him to draw near, and he shall approach unto me: for who is this that engaged his heart to approach unto me? saith the Lord."

Jeremiah 33:26

"Then will I cast away the seed of Jacob and David my servant, so that I will not take any of his seed to be **rulers** over the seed of Abraham, Isaac, and Jacob: for I will cause their captivity to return, and have mercy on them."

Jeremiah 51:46

"And lest your heart faint, and ye fear for the rumour that shall be heard in the land; a rumour shall both come one year, and after that in another year shall come a rumour, and violence in the land, **ruler** against **ruler**."

Lamentations 5:8

"Servants have **ruled** over us: there is none that doth deliver us out of their hand."

Ezekiel 19:11

"And she had strong rods for the sceptres of them that bare **rule**, and her stature was exalted among the thick branches, and she appeared in her height with the multitude of her branches."

Ezekiel 19:14

"And fire is gone out of a rod of her branches, which hath devoured her fruit, so that she hath no strong rod to be a sceptre to **rule**. This is a lamentation, and shall be for a lamentation."

Daniel 11:3

"And a mighty king shall stand up, that shall **rule** with great dominion, and do according to his will."

Daniel 11:4

"And when he shall stand up, his kingdom shall be broken, and shall be divided toward the four winds of heaven; and not to his posterity, nor according to his dominion which he **ruled**: for his kingdom shall be plucked up, even for others beside those."

Daniel 11:5

"And the king of the south shall be strong, and one of his princes; and he shall be strong above him and have **dominion**; his dominion shall be a great dominion."

Daniel 11:39

"Thus shall he do in the most strong holds with a strange god, whom he shall acknowledge and increase with glory: and he shall cause them to **rule** over many and shall divide the land for gain."

Daniel 11:43

"But he shall have **power** over the treasures of gold and of silver, and over all the precious things of Egypt: and the Libyans and the Ethiopians shall be at his steps."

Joel 2:17

"Let the priests, the ministers of the Lord, weep between the porch and the altar, and let them say, Spare thy people, O Lord, and give not thine heritage to reproach, that the heathen should **rule** over them: wherefore should they say among the people, Where is their God?"

Micah 5:2

"But thou, Bethlehem Ephratah, though thou be little among the thousands of Judah, yet out of thee shall he come forth unto me that is to be **ruler** in Israel; whose goings forth have been from of old, from everlasting."

Habakkuk 1:14

"And makest men as the fishes of the sea, as the creeping things, that have no **ruler** over them?"

Zechariah 6:13

"Even he shall build the temple of the Lord; and he shall bear the glory and shall sit and **rule** upon his throne; and he shall be a priest upon his throne: and the counsel of peace shall be between them both."

www.ingramcontent.com/pod-product-compliance
Lightning Source LLC
Chambersburg PA
CBHW070320010526
44107CB00004B/363